Praise for *Life with Pop:*
Lessons on Caring for an Aging Parent

"Dr. Spring's beautiful writing transports us. You will feel better knowing it's not just you who is ashamed and awed by the challenges of caring for elderly parents. I loved this book and recommend it to everyone who is beginning or ending the journey. It's a lonesome valley, made less lonesome by this remarkable book."

  —RICHARD C. SCHWARTZ, PH.D., founder of Internal Family Systems therapy

"This is more than just a book about caring for an aging parent. It is about human endurance, discovering who we really are, questioning our core values, seeing our future through a magnifying glass, and coming face-to-face with excruciating life-and-death choices. In absorbing detail, the author takes us on this soul-changing journey, one that is bound to move and inspire her readers."

  —PEGGY PAPP, MSW, senior supervisor at the Ackerman Institute for the
  Family

"Tender, powerful, bluntly honest, *Life with Pop* explores the extraordinary personal challenges and moments of grace that come with caring for an aging parent. I was a long-distance son, loving but not present. Janis's book showed me with sharp clarity some of the joy I missed and some of the burden I was spared. Rather than inducing guilt and regret, though, it filled me with compassion for all families taking this last walk together. It was a gift to me. Read it. It will be a gift to you."

  —DAVID TREADWAY, PH.D., coauthor of *Home Before Dark: A Family's First*
  Year with Cancer

LIFE WITH POP

Lessons on Caring for an Aging Parent

JANIS ABRAHMS SPRING, Ph.D.

with MICHAEL SPRING

AVERY

a member of

Penguin Group (USA) Inc.

New York

Published by the Penguin Group
Penguin Group (USA) Inc., 375 Hudson Street, New York, New York 10014, USA • Penguin Group (Canada),
90 Eglinton Avenue East, Suite 700, Toronto, Ontario M4P 2Y3, Canada (a division of Pearson Canada Inc.) •
Penguin Books Ltd, 80 Strand, London WC2R 0RL, England • Penguin Ireland, 25 St Stephen's Green,
Dublin 2, Ireland (a division of Penguin Books Ltd) • Penguin Group (Australia), 250 Camberwell Road,
Camberwell, Victoria 3124, Australia (a division of Pearson Australia Group Pty Ltd) • Penguin Books India
Pvt Ltd, 11 Community Centre, Panchsheel Park, New Delhi–110 017, India • Penguin Group (NZ),
67 Apollo Drive, Rosedale, North Shore 0632, New Zealand (a division of Pearson New Zealand Ltd) •
Penguin Books (South Africa) (Pty) Ltd, 24 Sturdee Avenue, Rosebank, Johannesburg 2196, South Africa

Penguin Books Ltd, Registered Offices: 80 Strand, London WC2R 0RL, England

"By a Departing Light" is reprinted by permission of the publishers and the trustees of Amherst College from
The Poems of Emily Dickinson: Variorum Edition, Ralph W. Franklin, ed. Cambridge, Mass.: The Belknap Press of
Harvard University Press, copyright © 1998 by the President and Fellows of Harvard College. Copyright © 1951,
1955, 1979, 1983 by the President and Fellows of Harvard College.

Most Avery books are available at special quantity discounts for bulk purchase for sales promotions, premiums,
fund-raising, and educational needs. Special books or book excerpts also can be created to fit specific needs. For
details, write Penguin Group (USA) Inc. Special Markets, 375 Hudson Street, New York, NY 10014.

Library of Congress Cataloging-in-Publication Data

Spring, Janis Abrahms.
  Life with pop : lessons on caring for an aging parent / Janis Abrahms Spring with Michael Spring.
    p.   cm.
  ISBN 978-1-58333-342-6
  1. Aging parents—Care.   2. Older people—Care.   3. Caregivers.   I. Spring, Michael.   II. Title.
HQ1063.6.S67   2009   2008046397
362.6092—dc22
[B]

Printed in the United States of America
10 9 8 7 6 5 4 3 2 1

Book design by Michelle McMillian

All of the patients described in this book are composites. Extensive details have been changed to protect the confi-
dentiality and privacy of my patients and research participants. The patient cases in the book are emotionally real,
but no case corresponds to any actual person, living or dead.

All patients' names have been changed to protect privacy.

While the author has made every effort to provide accurate telephone numbers and Internet addresses at the time
of publication, neither the publisher nor the author assumes any responsibility for errors, or for changes that occur
after publication. Further, the publisher does not have any control over and does not assume any responsibility for
author or third-party websites or their content.

To the sweet memory of our parents,

Dolly and Louie Lieff

and Muriel and Sol Spring

Author's Note

I've come to believe there are two types of people in the world: those who have cared for an aging parent and those who haven't.

Caregiving is a life-altering, life-defining experience. I had no idea, when I signed up for the job, of the range and intensity of emotion it would draw from me. Now I do. It has been a joy and an imposition. A blessing and a curse. A little of both. A lot of both.

Life with Pop is a book of reflections drawn from the five years I spent watching over my elderly father. Often I speak in the voice of a guilt-ridden, overwhelmed, loving daughter shepherding her declining dad through sometimes green, sometimes gray pastures. At other times, I step into my professional role as a clinical psychologist and address patients with caregiving issues of their own. I hope that in listening to our confessions, you'll find a language for what you're experiencing and feel less crazy, helpless, and alone.

I'd like to thank some special people who contributed to this book. First and foremost is my husband and coauthor, Michael. This is the third book we've written together. Who knew it was going to be so hard?

"Go deeper," you scribbled so annoyingly in the margins of my manuscript.

"Do you think I'm deliberately trying to be superficial?" I growled.

In the end, you pushed me to keep my emotions honest, and never to use three words when two will do. I love you for your uncluttered style and for your calm, sweet, steady disposition, so like my father's.

Max and Aaron, Louie's cherished grandsons, and Ali, Declan, Robin, and Evan—I love you, too, and I'm grateful to you for tolerating my absence, first while I was caring for Dad, then while I wrote this book. Your encouragement and affection helped keep me going.

Joel, my dear brother, thank you for being a loving presence in Dad's life, and in mine. Janice, Sue, and Mort—you opened your hearts to Dad and brought comfort to his final years.

Phoebe, you were conceived the week Dad died. How wonderful to see his spirit live on in you.

Beth Vessel, my agent, you gave me invaluable direction and support. Lucia Watson, my sharp and sensitive editor at Avery Penguin, you recognized the need for an unsanitized account of the caregiving experience and gave me the chance to tell it.

Israel Stein, rabbi emeritus at Rodeph Sholom Congregation in Bridgeport, Connecticut, your wise, fiery, compassionate vision continues to captivate and inspire me.

Dad's aides and doctors, the hospice staff at Hartford Hospital, and the Summerwood community, I owe you a debt of gratitude for a thousand acts of kindness.

I'm also grateful to you, my patients, for putting a human face on the struggle of millions of caregivers to do the right thing by their parents: to find them an appropriate living facility; to resolve sibling rivalries; to make irreversible healthcare and end-of-life decisions for them; to cope with their ingratitude and mistrust or, just as difficult, their goodness and love—all at a time when you're feeling panicky and depleted yourself. I learned so much from you.

For everyone consumed by the needs of an elderly parent, may this book replenish your spiritual reserves. When times are tough and you fall short, may it teach you to topple your inner critic and treat yourself with the compassion and understanding you deserve. May it also prepare you for your own old age and help you become the type of person who brings out the best in those who care for you.

I wish you and your parents courage and strength and many blessed memories, as you make this extraordinarily ordinary, illuminating journey.

By a departing light
We see acuter, quite,
Than by a wick that stays.
There's something in the flight
That clarifies the sight
And decks the rays.
— EMILY DICKINSON

CONTENTS

LIFE WITH POP

DAYS OF AWE
October 3, 2005

Sunset, erev Rosh Hashanah. The start of the Jewish New Year, a time of repentance and renewal. In synagogue, I slip into a pew beside Michael and take his hand. He has been a loving partner, patiently supporting my involvement with Dad. I feel terrible, neglecting him and everyone else in my life, including my kids. I try to show interest in their lives, but often I'm too preoccupied. My friends? Who has time for friends? I hope they'll forgive me for being so out of touch. I'm worn out with anxiety and the constant pressure of being in charge. Dear Pop. How could one old man create so much work? I close my eyes and pray for a spiritual transfusion to get me through whatever lies ahead.

Rabbi Stein steps up to the bimah. "I'd like to talk tonight about the noble and challenging work of caregivers," he begins. "It is hard, almost unimaginably hard, to be a caregiver, for when you care for someone whose mind and body have been greatly diminished by illness, your life is consumed by it, and there is little relief and respite. You must struggle against exhaustion, against self-pity, against resentment, and a host of other emotions that no one who has not gone through what you are going through can ever even begin to understand."

The rabbi runs his eyes over the congregation. I'm stunned by his timing.

"You know who you are. You wear no badges, receive no plaques. There are no tribute dinners in your honor. We give medals to soldiers who show courage in adversity, but not to those ordinary people who sacrifice their lives, caring for the sick and the old. I can only imagine how much you must wish that at least once in your life someone would recognize what you are going through, someone would speak to your haggard souls, so you would not feel so terribly alone. My parents had a wonderful expression. They used to say: 'No one should ever find out how much he is capable of enduring.'

"There is an alternative, of course. You could quit. You could abandon the one you are caring for. But you don't. You muster up the physical and emotional stamina that caregiving requires, day after day, sometimes year after year, and hold on fiercely, caring for someone for whom you may have had, not always love, but sometimes ambivalent and complex feelings. This is heroism of the highest order."

I look around the synagogue. The woman in front of me stands beside a shrunken old man. Her father? He's half her height, barely able to stand. Where is his wife—her mother? Where are her brothers and sisters? I watch as the man gives in to his tremors and reaches for his seat. She helps him lower himself down. Across the aisle, an elderly woman— she can hardly walk herself—pushes her husband in a wheelchair toward the bathroom. Everywhere, people caring for people. Everywhere, empty seats and wet eyes.

It feels good hearing someone give a language, a legiti-
macy, to what I'm experiencing. I'm proud to have cared for
Dad these past five years, defending the sanctity of life. And
yet I'm so bone-tired, shielding him from death. Will I see
this through, or cave in to my exhaustion and throw in the
towel? Am I one of Rabbi Stein's heroes, or a quitter, un-
equal to the task?

Dad lies helplessly in the hospital, trusting I'll do what's best
for him. But I'm paralyzed. If I choose to let him die, how
will I know I'm acting on *his* behalf, not on mine? Will my
fatigue tip the scale, getting the best of me? Is this how the
story ends: the weak, well-intentioned daughter putting her
father to rest because *she*'s weary?

A GOOD WOMAN DIES
October 21, 2000

The call comes early from Mom's oncologist: "I'm very
sorry. Your mother passed away this morning."

I'm sitting in my parents' kitchen with my frail, gentle,
eighty-year-old father. My husband, Michael, is filling in for
Mom, making weak decaf, just the way Dad likes it. I'm terrified by what I'm about to unleash.

"Dad, that was the doctor. He has bad news. Mom just
died."

Dad stares into a bowl of hot cereal, his eyes spilling over with tears. I rush over and wrap my arms around his soft, hulking, bearlike frame. I can't tolerate his pain. There's no time to know my own.

My mind races. Call my brother. Call the kids. Call the undertaker—how do we get Mom's body from Florida to Connecticut? Write an obituary. Where will it appear?

Dad is a quiet, unassuming man. He tends to lead with humor, not with demands. But today he makes his wishes known. "I want an announcement in the paper," he says resolutely. "I want it to say, a good woman died. A *good* woman."

Dad has suffered from a catalog of physical ailments over the years—a massive coronary at age forty-two, transient ischemic attacks (TIAs), bladder and prostate cancers, cataracts, malaria, high blood pressure, high cholesterol, pemphigus, an arthritic hip joint, tremors from Parkinson's. The list goes on and on. I hear my mother's voice, the one I heard throughout my childhood: "He can't take the pressure. He's going to have a heart attack." Her fears are now my own.

Somehow we stumble through the morning. Dad doesn't die, and I begin to think about the next step. Where is he going to live? Who's going to take care of him?

Mom asked me a year ago if she could move in with me "when the time comes." I answered with a joke that wasn't meant to be funny: "Forget it, Mom. You'll never live with me—ever." *I'm not a masochist or a saint.* "You'd drive me crazy. I love you, but my house isn't big enough for both of us."

Just to make sure she understood, just to drive the point home, I repeated, "Mom, I'm serious. Living with me is not an option, but I promise you this: I'll find you a great place to stay. I'll visit you often and make sure you're comfortable. You have my word."

The unimaginable has happened. Mom is dead. Dad, one of the sweetest, most helpless men I know, now turns to ask me a favor: "Can I come live with you?"

Kind, gentle Pop. Who never asks for anything. Who never interferes or gives advice. Who has loved me as purely as any child could wish. How can I deny him this one request?

But all I can think is, God forgive me, if he moves in with me, my life is finished. Mom always catered to him. I would, too—out of guilt, love, an overdeveloped sense of responsibility. I'd give everything and have no life of my own. *I'd become my mother.*

Michael stands behind me: "Of course your father wants to live with you. When your mother was alive, you had nothing but good times together. You took them to the flea market and out for hot pastrami. You drove them around and bought them cashmere sweaters. What's not to like? But that was twice a year. This is every day."

It was simple with my mother. I knew I'd never let her stay with me—our relationship was too contentious. It never occurred to me I'd have to turn away my father. Mom was supposed to outlive him. She was strong, invincible. He was the sick one.

Before the day ends, Dad brings the subject up again. This time he's crying, propositioning. He has thought it through. "I'll give you a hundred thousand dollars," he pleads with me. "You could build an addition to your house, and I'll live there. I won't bother you. I'll do errands for you.

I'll make dinner and bring your clothes to the cleaners. I won't cause you any trouble."

I swear. This is what he says, my father, begging me to save him from his loneliness, his terror. This man who gave me life and made me feel cherished. This man who, with my mother, logged in the hours, selling draperies and slipcovers in their modest fabric store to give me the opportunities they were denied. This man who doesn't know how to turn on a microwave or iron a shirt—begging me to allow him to be my personal valet. And I—the one so capable of taking care of him, the one with the lovely home and loving partner— am being tested and found wanting.

Am I that selfish, craving my own personal space, believing the quality of my life matters, too? Am I that bad? Can't I put Dad in a facility and still be an attentive, involved, loving child? Can't I be a good daughter and still set limits on how much I'm willing to sacrifice?

"No," I insist. "You can't live with me, Dad. As much as I love you, as much as I owe you. It won't work for me."

Dad looks at me and says nothing more.

It's the hardest conversation I've ever had.

Self-forgiveness

"Dear Dr. Spring," the e-mail begins. "I attended your workshop on forgiveness and am interested in your advice on caring for the elderly. May I ask you a question? How does a child forgive herself for putting a parent in a home? Even if the child is certain that her parent can't

manage alone anymore; even if family and friends support her a hundred percent, she is likely to agonize over
the decision and suffer from a crippling sense of guilt and
self-blame. And this is when the facility is decent and the
care is good."

"Dear Michelle," I write back. "You're describing a
child who can't forgive herself, even when she's done nothing wrong, certainly nothing malicious. She hates herself
for giving up the fight, for quitting, for not sacrificing
more. The parent complains, 'What am I doing here? I
want to go home. I want my life back. Can't I live with
you?' And the child castigates herself again.

"It's normal and appropriate for a child to feel guilty
when she has intentionally wronged someone and violated
her own code of decency. Guilt can be a wake-up call to
do better, to be better. But sometimes guilt is out of pro-
portion to the offense, and comes from an excessive sense
of responsibility. Love is confused with self-denial. When
a child can't allow herself any degree of selfishness, her
reward is often depression and even self-loathing.

"Self-forgiveness requires the child to accept her complicity in all the ways she has wronged her parents over
their lives and to redress the harm she has done. But
it also asks her to judge herself with the same gentle
and patient understanding she would offer a good friend.
She might ask herself, 'How would I react to someone
I liked and respected who told me that, after much self-
questioning, she decided to put her parent in a home?
Would I berate her for setting limits?' The caretaking
child needs to talk back to the harsh, recriminating voice

that tells her she's bad—bad for feeling so burned out, bad for craving her own personal space, bad for tending to her own needs and believing the quality of her *life matters, too.*

"Self-forgiveness also requires her to reclaim what she most values in herself and appreciate all that she has done—and continues to do—that's good and right for her parents. She must recognize not only how she falls short but how she extends herself to make her parents safe, comfortable, and happy.

"It's not all or nothing. You can be a good son or daughter and still set boundaries on how much of your resources you're willing to devote to your parents. You can be protective and compassionate toward them and also toward yourself. You can put your parents in a facility and still be an attentive, involved, loving child."

THE FUNERAL
October 24, 2000

It's a raw, thankless day at the Loyalty Lodge Cemetery in Bridgeport, Connecticut. A few close relatives and neighbors huddle under a canvas canopy, dodging an icy drizzle. Dad is the last of his generation; both of his brothers are gone. Most of my parents' friends now live in Florida—no one goes north for a funeral unless it's his own.

Dad sits front and center on a flimsy bridge chair, eyeing Mom's casket. For decades she nursed him from one chest pain, one cancer scare, to another, a strong bull of a woman, oblivious to her own aches and pains. If the world made sense, she'd be mourning him today.

Not long ago I bullied her into seeing a doctor. She was spending an uncharacteristic amount of time in bed, insisting that her greatest affliction was chronic constipation, nothing that a few pills couldn't cure. But a lifetime of smoking had finally caught up to her, and in six weeks she was dead.

Our family rabbi, Israel Stein, pins a black ribbon on Dad's chest and tears it. "With great love there is great loss," he says, gazing sympathetically into Dad's pale, rumpled face. "You can't love someone so much and not grieve deeply when you lose them."

Mom and Dad got engaged in their late twenties. It was 1944, the year that *Casablanca* was named best film and Bing Crosby's "I'll Be Seeing You" filled the airwaves. When Dad was drafted into the Army, Mom took a train across country to spend the weekend with him before his unit sailed off to the Philippines. Only love could have made her that daring. After the war they got married, and, except when he was hospitalized, she never slept away from him, not once in fifty-four years.

They were a couple, Dolly and Louie, a horse and carriage—Mom the horse, Dad the carriage. She ran the fabric store and he schmoozed with the customers. She was the miracle worker, keeping him alive; he was the grateful patient, defying death. Mom managed her anxiety by ironing and spraying the kitchen for ants. Dad managed his anxiety by playing golf and going fishing. Mom rarely criticized him. Dad rarely complained. She made him stuffed cabbage, and he made her smile. She made the beds and he played the saxophone and filled her heart with music. She talked and he listened. The only time I saw him lead her was on the dance floor, where he made her feel like his beautiful, graceful girl, his Dolly.

The rain beats down on a rusty garbage can overflowing with discarded plastic pots and wilted flowers, only steps from the grave. Mom would be mortified. What a dismal place to spend eternity: a flat, treeless expanse of rough grass and weeds, surrounded by a chain-link fence. What were my parents thinking when they bought these plots four decades ago? I'm sure nothing more complicated than the wish to spend forever in the company of family and friends.

Mom is lowered into the ground. I heave a shovelful of dirt on her coffin, fulfilling the obligation of the living to bury the dead. It's a refined but sensible box I chose for her: she would have been annoyed by anything more extravagant. "Save your money for a rainy day, Jan," she would have said. "It'll come."

What do I feel? Anxiety more than grief, regret more than love. Mom was so busy running the family and the store, she didn't have time for me, not the personal time I craved. Her shorthand way of parenting was to give advice, which often sounded like criticism. I wanted a friend to hang out with, someone to encourage me and take delight in me, but she counted on me not to add to her burden. For the most part, I complied.

The rain thickens. Dad huddles in his dark, wool-lined trench coat, too stunned for tears. Mom did everything for Dad. He was her mission, her charge. Now he's mine. My challenge today? To be there for Dad without being consumed by him; to show my love for him without abandoning myself.

HOME CARE
December 10, 2000

Dad is back in Florida. I tried to keep him in Connecticut, near me, but he insisted on returning to his Delray Beach condo. Who can blame him? If he can't live with me, he wants to be back in the sun. Why subject old bones to a howling New England winter? Why give up a bathing suit for boots and gloves?

Dad is making a life for himself. He retired his golf clubs a few months ago but still likes to putt on the clubhouse green. He drives during daylight hours, ambles about haltingly without a cane, walks the water in the pool, plays bridge with the guys in the men's lounge, and eats enthusiastically—God bless his appetite.

There are times, though, when he simply can't function

alone. He would love to go to the movies at night but, as they say, a man needs a wife to drive him. Who will manage the late-night emergencies, never mind the laundry and medication? His apartment is on the second floor, reached by a steep flight of concrete steps, the color of flamingos. How long before he slips and falls?

I contact a home-care agency and arrange for an aide to spend a few hours every afternoon with Dad, running errands, fixing him dinner, but she never shows up. Her replacement talks Dad's ear off, so I let her go. I dismiss the next one, too, when she tries to hit him up for a loan. The fourth arranges to have her young children dropped off at Dad's apartment after school—Dad loves life, but not that much. The fifth spends her day in Dad's kitchen, reading the Bible. She reminds Dad that Jesus loves him, praise the Lord.

Home companion Number Six is bright and friendly but cooks an early dinner and leaves by five. I give her Mom's recipes, but she ignores them. Dad sits in his kitchen alone, nibbling on salted cod with hot pepper, cold and soggy because he can't operate the microwave. He's used to cold borscht with sour cream, or brisket with steamed broccoli—tastes as foreign to his caregiver as hers are to him.

Dad is becoming more and more isolated, walled up in his apartment, wed to his new bride, the TV. When I call, I often catch him napping.

Who am I kidding? Dad needs to get a life. This one's not working.

INDEPENDENT LIVING
February 8, 2001

Maybe a compromise can be reached. Maybe Dad can stay in Florida in a supportive adult community and I can be a loving, involved daughter, managing the details from Connecticut, fourteen hundred miles away. Mike and I fly south to scope out the options.

The first place we visit, an independent-living facility, is too independent for Dad. The residents are healthy and vigorous, and scurry from activity to activity—yoga, digital photography, mutual-fund investing. They discuss Philip Roth in a book club and learn how to roll a credible maki sushi in cooking class. They do their own wash. Dad couldn't even walk from the lobby to his apartment.

Our next stop, an assisted-living facility, is too assisted. Residents shuffle breathlessly down the corridors, clutching walkers, or sit diapered on outdoor patios in wheelchairs pushed by hired hands. The level of care is much higher here, but death lurks in every corner. The director, itching for a sale, pounces on our hesitation. "Just don't wait too long," she admonishes us. "Children often make that mistake, then they're hit with a crisis and there's no place for their parents to go. Most good facilities have a waiting list several months long."

She smells blood, the viper.

When Mom was hospitalized, I put down a deposit on an apartment in Summerwood, an independent-living facility in West Hartford, Connecticut, that would be opening soon. Dad knows the neighborhood intimately: we lived only minutes away. Dad could drive around, find his old barber, even shop at the Crown, an incomparable kosher supermarket right up the street. He has a few old friends who still live in town, the beginnings of a social life. Michael's sister, Sue, lives nearby. Most important, Michael and I live only an hour and fifteen minutes away.

I press Dad to try Summerwood for six months, promising not to sell his condo, perhaps just to rent it. If the cold gets to him, we'll figure out how to get him back south. With great reluctance, he puts himself in my hands.

In bringing Dad north, my life takes on a new focus. I give it a name. I call it, fondly, Pop, the Project.

SUMMERWOOD
February 28, 2001

Summerwood is a compact, cedar-shingled, three-story building set comfortably back from a quiet suburban road. A circular driveway cuts through a mottled lawn landscaped with young hydrangea bushes and old trees. A few residents huddle on an open porch, kibitzing, waiting for spring.

"I'm here to check out my father's new apartment," I tell the receptionist.

"Does he like Frank Sinatra?" she asks with a cheerful informality. "I'm hoping to play oldies-but-goodies on Sunday afternoons."

On the counter in front of her is a card for residents to sign. It says: "Wishing you sweet memories of your husband."

I've chosen a one-bedroom unit on the top floor, just off the elevator, an easy walk for Dad. The laundry room is only steps away. Who knows? He may learn to wash his shirts and socks someday.

Sunshine floods the apartment: a bright, empty space waiting to be filled. The walls are soft cream, the color of Dad's temperament—calm, unimposing. The bathroom has an oversize door for a wheelchair and a huge open shower. A single bed is all he needs now. Propped up on pillows, he can peer out the window at the tops of trees and enjoy the changing seasons. He can also look down at the parking lot and see me coming to visit him, bearing turkey pastrami and half-sour pickles.

Summerwood opened only a month ago but is already three-quarters full: about sixty residents have moved in, mostly women, and mostly Jewish, though not necessarily religious, ranging from their midseventies to nearly a hundred. A few share space with an ailing partner, but most live alone, their partners dead or living out their final days in nursing homes nearby.

Summerwood seems too good to be true. Except for the Sabbath, there are activities every day of the week: ceramics, painting, aerobics, bridge. The University of Hartford is right down the street, hosting concerts and cultural events, free to the elderly. Only minutes away is the Jewish Community Center with its exercise room and men's club. Not that Dad is going to play racquetball, but with help he could walk the shallow end of the indoor pool.

Dad gets transportation to medical appointments and access to a daytime nurse. Aides are available for hourly hire to bathe him and dispense medications. If he pushes the emergency button on his necklace, someone will come running. If he doesn't show up for meals, someone will find out why.

Summerwood serves two kosher meals a day, breakfast and dinner. Dad is far from kosher, but at least he'll recognize the food, and he can order a tuna fish on rye for lunch in the second-floor café if he's willing to fork over five bucks.

On the carpet by the window I place a hearty, two-foot Kentia palm plant. This will give the apartment some life. It will also give Dad something to care for and occupy his mind other than his aches and pains. We'll see whether he remembers to water it.

All things considered, the apartment looks great—cozy, familiar, manageable, fresh. I'll do my best to make it his home. I feel an optimism, a sense of control I haven't felt since Mom got sick. *Maybe it's going to work out. Maybe there's a chance it will be okay.*

The Hardware Store
March 1, 2001

I'm off to the local hardware store to buy a paper-towel dispenser. "It's for my elderly father's new apartment," I explain to the salesclerk.

"Will it go into drywall, wood, or plasterboard?" he asks.

"You're kidding," I respond, rolling my eyes. Who has time for this? Dad is coming north in ten days.

He catches my impatience: "After all the time your father has given you, you don't have five minutes to get this right?"

I can't figure out if this guy is an insensitive bastard or just a bit gruff. Maybe he has an aging relative of his own. Or maybe he's trying to help me and I'm too sensitive.

I decide to trust his motives and open myself to him. "My mother died, and I'm moving my dad into an independent-living home."

His face softens. "That's hard," he says. "Really hard."

He doesn't ask, "Why isn't your father moving in with *you?*" but I imagine that's what he's thinking. That's what *I'm* thinking.

I pick up a few lightbulbs, a wastebasket, some plastic liners. This is the easy part. Checking things off lists, managing details.

"Just remember," he calls out as I walk toward the door.

"What will help your father most is if you visit him once in a while."

His wisdom shakes me. I should give him my job as a clinical psychologist, as a grieving, guilt-ridden daughter.

Guilt and Sorrow

"My mother is a sick, old woman who doesn't have much to live for," Sally tells me in an e-mail. "She drags herself around with emphysema, sucking in the air. I manage her care—she's in an assisted-living facility—but I constantly feel I'm not doing enough. I'm an expert in guilt, but sometimes I wonder if I'm masking other feelings— like grief."

"Yes," I write back, assuming my most professional voice, "for someone like you, the dedicated child, guilt is the easier emotion, the stronger suit. You know it all too well. It's a welcome distraction from grief, which is less familiar, less comfortable. With guilt, you're the hammer, in control, competently pounding away at your perceived deficiencies. With grief, you're the anvil, helpless to fend off the blows of time."

"I wouldn't mind a good cry," Sally admits. "It would feel good."

"You've been so busy nursing your mother, maybe you haven't had the time or strength to grieve. You may worry that if you open the floodgates, you'll drown. But if you can't know sadness, you can't know love."

I wish her well and send her this poem by Robert Browning Hamilton:

I walked a mile with Pleasure,
She chattered all the way,
But left me none the wiser
For all she had to say.

I walked a mile with Sorrow
And ne'er a word said she;
But oh, the things I learned from her
When Sorrow walked with me.

SHALL WE DANCE?
March 18, 2001

On Sunday afternoons, Summerwood hosts a social for the residents. They gather in the community room around two o'clock and listen to music, nosh on cake, hum, whistle, sing, and perhaps—if their legs are willing—dance. Some residents retreat to their apartments, but most of them appreciate the company and jump at the chance to reconnect and recharge.

When I call to say good night, Dad tells me he joined the party today. "The girl at the desk—Jean, the one with the big glasses—put on some Frank Sinatra," he says, barely able to control his pleasure. "She came over to me and said, 'Come on, Mr. Lieff. Dance with me!' 'Dance!' I told her. 'I can hardly walk.' But, Jan, guess what? I danced! Pretty good for an old cocker."

"That's great, Dad!" I say. And mean it. I could kiss Jean for bringing Dad back to life.

I hang up as waves of memories wash over me. Tomorrow is Mom's birthday. She would be eighty-one. How she and Dad loved to dance together. When my brother, Joel, and I were kids, we would take family trips to Miami and stay at the Fontainebleau, one of the big, splashy hotels on the beach. We spent our afternoons around the pool, taking dance lessons, then changed into our fancy clothes and dined in the hotel's shimmering ballroom while a live orchestra played big-band tunes. It was a kick, dancing with Dad or Joel, but I was happiest just sitting at the table, sipping a Shirley Temple, watching Dad swoop Mom up in his arms. They were dazzling—Mom with her coiffed silver blond hair, Dad with his deep tan and white linen jacket, which Mom carefully chose for him. Cha-cha-ing across a polished floor, they looked elegant and sexy to me, like Latino movie stars. Oh, did they have fun.

And now Dad is being asked to take his first step with a receptionist in a strange new home. To begin to move his feet and dance again. To let life in. It may be too early. I hope it's not too late.

A Fraternity of Men
April 24, 2001

A facility like Summerwood, it turns out, is a great place for old men, providing them with food and friendship. Without this community, they would be condemned to their homes or apartments, clutching their remote controls, too proud or awkward to reach out to others.

Dad is now part of a men's group that gathers every night at the same window table for dinner. Promptly at six-fifteen, Sam, ninety-three, knocks twice on Dad's door and accompanies him to the dining room, where they meet up with Murray, ninety-two, and Dave, eighty-seven.

It is a disparate crew. Sam, a short, slight man with white hair cropped close to his craggy skull, dresses straight from the Army & Navy store. His no-nonsense clothes are made to last—and, given the way he looks on most days, he has gotten his money's worth. In a former life Sam was a postal worker who never married and passed along a good share of his paycheck to his family, including a younger sister who, at ninety, lives alone in Hartford. Sam is self-educated, sharp, informed. He is also difficult and argumentative. What's harder to know—what's not immediately apparent from his gruff demeanor—is that he's a wonderful friend to Dad. How can I not love him? He has looked after Dad from the day he arrived, cutting his food when his hands shake too much to hold a knife, and signing him up for performances of *Grease* at the local high school and lectures on Frank Gehry.

Despite his age, Sam is in great physical shape, needing glasses only for reading, and walking without a cane. Every day he circles the property until he reaches his goal, a mile and a half. He's just as disciplined when it comes to his diet, carefully restricting his alcohol, fat, and cholesterol.

Murray, a large, lumbering man with pitted skin, is also one of the privileged few at Summerwood who can walk upright without assistance. A corporate accountant in his prime, he moved here when his wife died. As Jewish geography would have it, she was related to the woman my son is dating, making Dad and Murray virtual relatives. Murray dresses differently than Sam—spiffier, sportier—and owns a closet full of colored windbreakers with zippered fronts—yellow, royal blue, powder blue, beige. He wears them with matching trousers and golf caps, even though he doesn't play golf.

Dave is a bit younger than Murray and Sam, but the frailest. His wife lives at the Hebrew Home, her mind blanched by Alzheimer's. She stopped knowing him years ago, but he still visits her every day, a testament to his sweet disposition and solid character. Dave never complains about his Parkinson's, but he moves with tiny, mincing steps as though he's about to fall. Once a successful architect, he now struggles to do the simplest tasks, like buttoning his shirt.

After dinner, the four guys shuffle up to the second-floor activity room to watch the news or sports. They're huge fans of the UConn girls' basketball team. The ladies monopolize the big-screen TV downstairs in the lounge, where they watch their favorite programs, usually sitcoms. The women are into relationships, the men into games— nothing different from the world outside.

"What do you talk about?" I ask Dad.

"Sam and Murray fight like cats and dogs. Sometimes they can get really nasty."

"Yeah? About what?"

"Oh, politics, mostly. The other night Sam said we should stay the hell out of Afghanistan. He said we've got enough problems at home. Murray told Sam, 'Sam, you've got your head in the sand.'"

"What did Dave say?"

"Dave, you know, is a gentleman with a lot of health problems. He just kept chewing his meatballs."

"And you?"

"I don't like it when things get ugly, but I've got to admit, I learn something new every day. Sam's smart. He still reads the paper, cover to cover. And Murray has a phenomenal memory. You can't believe what he knows—he can play every Broadway song on the piano, by heart. And he's a hell of a historian. Dinner can be very entertaining."

Dad pauses. "Last night, Sam and Murray were at each other's throats. It was a little much. I said, 'Okay, okay, that's enough. Have some pudding,' and they settled down. They're pretty good about trying to get along. You know, Jan, when you live in a place like Summerwood, you can't make too many enemies. It's not as if we have a lot of options."

In this sea of women, the four men have banded together.

In an earlier life, they probably would never have jelled, but necessity has made them buddies, teaching them, perhaps for the first time, to reach out and accept their dependence on other men. It's a new team sport called Life without Partners.

"LAST NIGHT, WHEN WE WERE YOUNG"
April 25, 2001

Wednesday afternoon is open house at the Senior Center in West Hartford Center for anyone who loves to dance. Dad reluctantly agrees to check it out with me. *If dancing has made the man happy, let's try it.*

We drive into town and use Dad's disabled driver's permit to snag a parking spot, one of the few privileges of old age. Dad extricates himself from the car and, defying his hip replacement and early Parkinson's, tosses his cane on to the front seat.

The elevator climbs slowly, haltingly, and empties us into a large, soft-lit room packed with seniors, seventy, eighty of them, mostly in pairs, shuffling their bent bodies across a speckled-linoleum floor. Ella sings: "Last night, when we were young . . ." I help Dad to a cup of sugary lemonade and sit down with him against the wall. It's all new to him. To us.

A few minutes pass. "You want to dance?" I ask.

"I'm too old, Jan."

"Come on. Let's try. We're here."

Hesitantly, he follows me on to the dance floor. As couples bob and sway around us, Dad wraps a hand around my waist, an innocent gesture that suddenly feels too intimate. Billie Holiday cries out, "Willow weep for me ..." Dad does a complicated step I've never been able to follow. I keep making wrong turns, crunching his toes.

We stumble through a few more numbers, then Dad says, "Come on, Sher, let's pack it in," and we head back to the car. We tried to have fun, but it wasn't fun. It was work, awkward and melancholy. It's as clear to Dad as it is to me: when it comes to dancing, I'll never fill in for Mom.

We turn to each other and exchange tired smiles, relieved to be back in the sunshine and fresh air.

I load Dad into the car and snap on his seat belt. "How about a strawberry ice-cream cone, Pop?"

"That's good."

This is going to take time, I realize. There's no quick fix, no two-step to quell the ache in our hearts.

They say a mother is only as happy as her most unhappy child. Maybe it's fair to say a daughter is only as happy as her most unhappy parent. Since Dad is the only one I have left, his mood is mine.

Elizabeth Park
May 25, 2001

Dad and I go to Elizabeth Park to get outside, eat our chicken-salad sandwiches, and enjoy the fresh air. We find a shaded park bench in the rose gardens, which we claim as our own.

I unpack our picnic and begin to wolf down my sandwich. I notice Dad peering into his. "Look at the colors in this sandwich," he remarks, mostly to himself.

I look into my sandwich for the first time. Bits of red tomato, magenta onion, green celery, mauve grapes, amber walnuts. How great to take a moment to notice the colors in the world. Next month, the roses will bloom. Will I stop to notice?

I slow down to let my muscles uncoil. More questions. What is the point of this visit? What is the point of my life? What makes today worth living? Why do I pack so much into a day? Dad, my Jewish Buddha, practices mindfulness intuitively. I should take a lesson from him. Be here—now. Be aware of the miracle of your breath; the smells, sights, sounds around you.

In order to ground myself in the here and now, I dwell on the contingency of things, the fragility of our existence. "Dad won't be here forever," I tell myself. "I won't be here forever. Don't take this time for granted."

I wish there were another way. I wish I could appreciate this ordinary moment for what it is, and still maintain a sense of specialness and awe. I wish I didn't need to be wowed, or rattled, to be impressed.

I look over at Dad, my aging father, sitting quietly on the bench. He seems content, just breathing the air. He doesn't need to remind himself the end is near to enjoy our visit. He doesn't need to terrorize himself with the elusiveness of time to value it. Of course, there may be more percolating inside him than I realize, but if I asked him, "How do you do it? How do you lend yourself so instinctively to the day?" I'm sure he'd say, "Does it have to be that complicated?"

For now, I put my angst, my tiresome angst, aside.

"Hey, Pop, how 'bout we go feed the ducks?"

"That's good," he says.

I'm grateful to Dad, who teaches me to awaken my senses and inhale life, and exhale the toxins, the tumult I create.

NAME-CALLING
May 30, 2001

When my father is sick or troubled, I call him Dad, just as I did as a kid. He was always Louie to others. Label to his Jewish friends. Labe to my mother.

When I walk into his apartment and see him sitting in his big green chair, smiling up at me, I toss up my arms, *Fiddler on the Roof* style, and croon, "The poppa! The poppa!" It's an intimate dance that makes my day.

On the phone, I greet him with "Hi, Pop!" and he answers, drolly, "Why, Janis Sheri." I always hated my middle name—Sheri—but coming from him, it sounds just right.

There's something about calling him Pop that makes me smile. I suppose it's because he's so damn uneffervescent, and cute.

Pop. Poppa. Janis Sheri. Terms of endearment. As affectionate, perhaps, as "I love you."

A PERFECT FIT
June 10, 2001

There are few surprises in life. Each of us fills roles we were assigned from the day we were conceived. Dad was the baby in his family, the youngest of three brothers. His mother favored him and made excuses for him, covering his tracks to allow him to play golf when he should have been at school or working in his father's rag store. My mother carried on the tradition, cooking, cleaning, and running errands for the two of them. He never took this as his divine right, his male prerogative; he was always grateful. And Mom was grateful for his gratitude, happy to make him happy.

Now, at Summerwood, the ladies fuss over him, fixing his collar, adjusting his suspenders, making him batches of their finest fudge brownies. Dad brings out the maternal instinct in all of them.

And here, for better or worse, I come. Dad, never one to take charge, requires more and more assistance, and I, the doting, obliging daughter, can't say no. Dad needs me; I need to feel needed. There will always be people like Dad, and there will always be people like me, and somehow we will always find each other.

We're hooked, till death do us part.

The Responsible Child

I hear from Michelle again:

Dear Dr. Spring,

A few months ago I wrote and asked you how a child seized with guilt forgives herself for putting her parents in a home against their wishes. I have another question, this time about me.

My father died years ago. When my mother got too sick to be alone, I didn't want her to live with me, but I couldn't slam the door on her, so I took her in. My best friend, faced with the same options, moved her father into a nursing home without a shred of guilt. I don't get it. How do some people say no to their parents and feel okay about themselves? Frankly, I'm jealous.

I write back, Some children say no easily because they genuinely believe a facility is the best place for their parents. They point to such practical consider-ations as:

- **Safety:** *"My house is a death trap—too many steps, slippery floors, no walk-in shower."*
- **Physical Health:** *"My mother needs ongoing medical attention and daily services such as physical therapy, which are more accessible in a continuing-care facility."*
- **Finances:** *"My parents' health-care policies cover expenses—aides and therapy—only in a medical facility, not at home."*
- **Social and emotional health:** *"My dad would be isolated living with me. He's better off in the more animated social world of an adult community, with the promise of new friends—perhaps even a new partner."*

Other children—the ones who are more self-serving than you—put their parents in a facility not because it's a better option for their parents but because it's a better option for themselves. They do this guilt-free, citing such personal factors as:

- *"I work at home and need privacy and quiet."*
- *"I have kids who require my full attention."*
- *"My marriage can't withstand the stress."*
- *"My mother is allergic to Milkshake, the cat. And Milkshake stays."*
- *"My father is demanding beyond belief, too difficult to have around full-time."*

Michelle responds, So why are some people more guilt-free?

Genetics may play a role. Some people are born takers: When they say "me," they feel right. Others are born givers: When they say "me," they feel dirty, cheap, wrong. Life experiences also shape us. If your grandmother lived with you during your childhood, and she was a positive, loving influence, you may today want to invite your mother into your home and give your kids the same rich, intergenerational experience you enjoyed. If your grandmother lived with you and everyone suffered—your mother, who ran herself ragged; your father, who felt abandoned; and you, who felt starved for attention—you may grow up resentful and be loath to subject your family to the same intrusion. Or—and this is where it gets complicated—you may find yourself replicating the same overly responsible, self-depriving pattern you were forced to exhibit as a child, and take your mother in because you can't put yourself first.

Most of us try to make a thoughtful choice, balancing care for our parents against care for ourselves, but there is no categorically right choice. It's not right to bring our parents into our home; it's not right to put them in a facility. The battle may seem to take place between our needs and theirs, but often it's waged inside us. Some people would like to think of themselves as selfless and all-loving, but when faced with the extraordinarily consuming task of caring for an elderly parent in their home, they refuse to accept the burden. Others would like to think of themselves as having a healthy degree of narcissism, but don't have the heart, the disposition, to act on their own behalf, and move their parents into a facility. The process of deciding where to place them forces us to grapple with our deepest values and discover who we are. It's a wrenching experience, because we not only confront our mother or father, we confront ourselves.

    Sincerely,

    Dr. Spring

TRANSITIONS
July 8 and 15, 2001

"I'm the youngest person at Summerwood," Dad announces. He's not a whiner by nature, but I hear his complaint: "What am I doing with all these old people? I don't belong here."

Dad is right, age-wise; at eighty-one, he *is* one of the youngest at Summerwood. Many residents are over ninety. Most of them, however, are far more vigorous. I could remind Dad that age doesn't necessarily correlate with health—he's living proof of this—but why burden him with the truth?

Dad's lament falls between comical and sad. This place is perfect for him—he just can't see it. No one else feels at home here, either. No matter how bent over, how gnarled and twisted they look today, their image of themselves dates back to an earlier era.

There's an unspoken competition among the residents. Those who walk with canes feel superior to those who get pushed in wheelchairs. Those, like Sam and Murray, who walk without canes are the leaders of the pack. Is it any wonder Dad parks his walking stick inside his apartment before stepping out into the hall?

At breakfast, a new resident approaches our table and introduces herself.

"Hi," she greets us warmly. "My name is Evelyn Bernstein. Are you Louie's daughter?"

"I am. I'm happy to meet you."

"Your father's a very sweet man," she says enthusiastically. "I'm trying to get him to take a ceramics class with me on Tuesdays." *This is good; already she has volunteered to be on Dad's entertainment committee.*

Evelyn seems like a nice lady, pleasantly dressed in a powder blue terry-cloth jogging suit and white Top-Siders, friendly, and very chatty. Her hair is almond brown, gray at the roots. Tortoiseshell reading glasses hang from a beaded cord around her neck, and her cheeks glow from a recent application of rouge. Her figure is still intact, curvy even. She stands erect and walks without a cane. Instantly, my mood perks up. *Company for Dad, maybe even a prospective bride.*

After breakfast, while Dad is in the bathroom, I seek Evelyn out in the lobby. She has been at Summerwood for two weeks.

"How's it going?" I ask.

"My husband died eight years ago," she tells me, which is where many of the residents' stories begin. "We lived in a condo about five miles from here. I adjusted and made a good life for myself. Our apartment was perfect for me, with high ceilings. I made myself dinner—I'm a good cook—or went out with friends. I even had my own garden. And I drove my own car. But I started having problems with my rotator cuff and had to give it all up. My kids worried about my being stuck alone in the apartment—I started skipping meals—so voilà, here I am."

Independent-living facilities are like quicksand—step inside and it's a steady and irreversible slide to the grave. Understandably, most people don't choose to come here. The decision is made for them when their lives take a turn for the worse. Ironically, it's when they can no longer live independently that they check in. And so the move is associated with grief and loss—loss of mobility and freedom, loss of loved ones, loss of youth, loss of health, loss of hope for a better future. The next step is an assisted-living facility, another name for a nursing home.

As Dad and I head upstairs to his rented space on the third floor, he mumbles, "I had a good life in Florida."

I hear Dad's sorrow and ache for him. I ache for Evelyn, too. No one wants to sit alone on the sidelines, watching others play the game. No one wants to be plucked out of a world of children and family and consigned to a home for the elderly. Who is there to pass their wisdom on to? To coddle and spoil? To make them feel valued and loved? Summerwood, no matter how good it gets, can't compete with what they had before.

At breakfast a week later, Dad and his male buddies engage in one of the great sports of the day, finding fault with Summerwood.

Sam, the spokesman, reels me into the conversation: "Can you believe we spend seventeen dollars a night for dinner, and they haven't figured out how to use the broiler yet? Last night, the fish was fried, soaked in oil." He surveys the room. "These people are old and sick. They're watching their cholesterol and weight. They don't need fried fish."

It's Murray's turn next. "Janis, can you believe the elevator got stuck yesterday? We had to wait in the lobby and couldn't get up to our rooms for two hours."

Dad chimes in. "I was dying to take a nap."

"They took us for ice cream in the van," Dave adds, "but it doesn't have a bathroom."

I start to defend Summerwood but stop myself. The villain is not Summerwood but life itself, and time, which drains us all. Complaining, of course, is one way of demanding respect and accountability, of saying no to the slurs and obloquies of old age. Though their universe is shrinking, the elderly still assert, "Don't judge me by what you see today."

We step into Dad's apartment. Sunlight pours through the open window, framing a fireworks display of cherry blossoms. The place smells clean, looks comfortable and attractive. Dad drops down into his green recliner, clicks on the TV, and turns to the stock market news. I head into the kitchen to prepare a new weekly medication chart. Dad's life is not so bad, I remind myself, all things considered.

But that's easy for me to say. I'm the one with the loving partner and the loving home. *I don't have to live here.*

The Podiatrist
July 16 and 20, 2001

"What does it cost to get a manicure?" Dad asks the receptionist at a local nail salon.

"Are you a senior citizen?"

"Don't bullshit me," Dad replies good-naturedly.

"Okay, ten dollars."

I leave Dad off and return when he's done. The manicurist has cut his fingernails down to the bleeding flesh. As we shuffle back to the car, Dad says, "I told her I wanted them short, but this is ridiculous."

"How are your toenails?" I ask.

"Their time has come. But I can't reach down that far."

"Summerwood has a manicurist who comes in every other week. Do you want me to make an appointment? It's twenty-five dollars."

"You're kidding," Dad replies. "There's a doctor on Asylum Avenue who takes Medicare and only charges fifteen. All the guys go to him."

"Okay, I'll take you next time I'm here."

The following week we walk into the doctor's office and are greeted by chaos and filth: chairs stained and torn, scattered papers, crumpled magazines, Styrofoam cups half-filled with brown sludge. A Dalmatian roams from room to room, lapping water from a red plastic bowl in a back office.

The doctor leads us into his examining room, seats Dad on a worn leather chair, pumps it into the air, and proceeds to clip his toenails with what look like dull, unsterilized utensils. The sink, streaked with iodine, is a repository of used gauze pads and clippings from previous patients.

I caution the doctor, "Please don't cut his toenails too short."

Mission accomplished, I hand over Dad's Medicare information and a fifteen-dollar co-payment. In the car, Dad and I have a good laugh.

"Pop," I say, shaking my head, "never, never again. This guy is dangerous."

"But cheap!" Dad chirps.

"Yeah, cheap. But did you see the toenail droppings in the sink?"

"You know, my friend Izzy tells me the doctor is an Orthodox Jew and isn't allowed to throw away toenails. He has to bury them in the ground. Maybe that's why they're there."

"That's good, Dad," I answer. "Next time, for ten dollars more, we'll try the lady at Summerwood."

Surprise, surprise. A week later, Dad develops an ingrown toenail, courtesy of the butcher, the Medicare podiatrist. I set up an appointment, this time with a foot doctor named Dr. Foote, recommended by Dad's internist. The appointment starts out well: her office is sparkling. After examining Dad, she asks, "Do you want me to remove the toenail or simply treat the problem?" Dad looks to me for the answer.

"How do we think about that?" I ask her.

"If I remove it, it's more extensive surgery, but it's more likely to grow back right. If I just treat the problem, it's likely to appear again."

Well, it depends on how long I think Dad will live.

"I'd say, let's do it right. How's that, Dad?"

"Okay," he says agreeably.

The podiatrist pokes a needle into Dad's toe and begins to carve away at the nail. I hold Dad's hand to provide company and support, but then my stomach begins to flop, and I retreat to the back of the room.

As the doctor pries off his toenail, Dad looks perfectly calm and comfortable, almost happy, to get the job done. "Who cuts your turkey at Thanksgiving?" he jokes.

Dr. Foote roars, reminding me that laughter is good medicine, too. It certainly provides better coverage than Medicare, and costs nothing.

ESTEE
August 9, 2001

Dad and I join his next-door neighbor, Estee, for breakfast.

"Hi, Estee," Dad says.

"Who's that?" she asks. "Louie?"

"And Janis, Louie's daughter," I answer.

Estee looks agitated today. Her wiry, steel-gray hair is uncombed, and her hand grips a tissue. A yellowish goo pools in the corner of one eye.

I walk over to the buffet to get Dad some hot cereal and prunes. When I return, tears are dripping down Estee's face.

A woman at the next table whispers to her friend, "What's with her?" The friend shakes her head as though to say, "Not good."

Estee holds back a sob and says to Dad and me, "Sometimes I can see a bit. Today, nothing."

A newcomer to Summerwood comes over and places her spotted hands gently on Estee's shoulder. "Estee, what would you like for breakfast?" she asks.

Another woman leans over to hug her and calls out cheerfully, "Estee, who am I?"

"Florie?"

"Yes!" Florie's voice resonates with delight. "You know me, Estee. You're okay."

I sit and watch. My eyes, too, are moist. I'm touched by the compassion these people show each other, day after day. A few, of course, turn their backs on their neighbors, ignoring their suffering, but most come forward and embrace whoever is struggling, offering help and encouragement. Their message is clear: "You're here with family. Don't be scared. We're all in this together."

THE PILL DISPENSER
September 30, 2001

The phone rings. It's the nurse from Summerwood. "Your dad took a whole day's worth of pills in one shot," she tells me. "He must have been confused."

"Oh, God. Should we get his stomach pumped?"

"I put him in bed. He seems better. But can you come?"

I look at my watch. Eight a.m. My first patient is about to arrive. "Sure, I'm on my way."

I weave in and out of traffic, trying to get a grip on more than just the steering wheel. What a hopeless, death-defying task, trying to keep the old on a regimen of pills.

Who can keep them all straight? There's Lipitor for cholesterol, Sinemet for Parkinson's, atenolol for angina, Ambien for insomnia, Plavix for heart attacks and strokes. Some pills need to be taken once a day, others three. Some work when the stomach's empty, others when it's full. Last week we discontinued one antibiotic and started another.

If the elderly could figure it out, they wouldn't need so much medication.

I buy Dad a plastic pill organizer with a maze of compartments, one row for each day of the week. Unfortunately, he can't open them or snap them shut. What clown, what sadist designed them?

I invest in an automatic pill dispenser. At the right time, a bell rings, a pill falls into a tray, and a digital voice cries out, "Please take your medication." If only Dad would do what he was told.

Dad could trek over to the nursing station and get the right dose four times a day, but who will remind him to go, and who will go after him when he doesn't show up? What Dad needs is a memory pill.

Poor, infuriating Dad. I've set him up to be independent, but he can't follow the simplest instructions, even though we've been over them a thousand times. I tape a sign to his front door in bold black letters—HAVE YOU TAKEN YOUR PILLS TODAY?—but he might as well be blind. I make a chart that any six-year-old could follow, but he forgets to check things off and by midweek some vials are half-full while others are empty. I want to scold him, but how can you berate

DAD'S MEDICATION CHART

	Breakfast		Lunch	Dinner		Bedtime
	Atenolol	Plavix	Sinemet	Sinemet	Lipitor	Ambien
Monday						
Tuesday						
Wednesday						
Thursday						
Friday						
Saturday						
Sunday						

someone for losing his memory? The scarier question is this: can anyone survive all these medications, even if they're properly dispensed? Does anyone know how they interact, how they confound each other's effects? Does anyone care?

Dad has a different doctor for every part of his body, and each doctor prescribes according to his specialty. One drug lowers his blood pressure but makes him light-headed and more likely to fall. Another improves his memory but raises his cholesterol. A third strengthens his bones but causes constipation. Who is coordinating this? Who is looking not at the leg, the heart, the lung, but the man?

There's no solution, none that's easy or inexpensive. For now, I arrange for a companion-care worker. She's not as pricey or skilled as a nurse—more like a babysitter—but she comes in each morning and gives Dad a shower and his morning medication, and gets him off on the right foot. We'll see how he manages the rest of the day on his own.

I need to feel useful, so I pull together a one-page report and send it to Dad's doctors, asking them to clip it to his chart. It lists the following:

- Dad's medications, and doses;
- His prescribing doctors and their phone numbers;
- His medical history;
- Insurance information;
- Emergency contact information.

I stuff a copy in Dad's wallet for emergencies, and tape another to the refrigerator door. Will this help? Or will it just help me feel less helpless?

As I leave Dad's apartment, I notice the pill bottles lined up on his kitchen counter like so many toy soldiers, staving off the enemy. We all know who's winning the battle.

Who Wants to Treat a Medicare Patient?

"What's your specialty?" I ask Carl, the handsome, thirty-something patient in my office.

"I'm a cardiologist," he says. *"In med school I wanted to be a gerontologist. I passed all the tests, but when it came time to pay for my certificate, I ripped up the check. I was deep in debt for my education and didn't think I could make a living caring for the old. Today, it's a group I want nothing to do with."* He smiles broadly and watches for my reaction.

"Why's that?"

"These people come into your office with a long history of chronic medical problems that can't be fixed—osteoporosis, diabetes, dementia. They expect you to talk to eight different specialists and review twenty-seven different medications. And, of course, they come to the appointment with three relatives, each with his own opinion about the direction the treatment should take. Then, just when you think you've got the case nailed down, a long-lost relative from the West Coast calls, threatening to sue you unless you do what they say."

"It takes a ton of time to coordinate care for the elderly," I acknowledge.

"And the truth is, with the way insurance companies reimburse you today, no doctor can afford to take them on. They require too much time. And the paperwork is ridiculous. You need a whole department just to process their claims."

"I know a lot of doctors don't accept Medicare."

"Our office made that 'call' last year. I know I sound harsh, but frankly the successful, better-trained doctors want patients who have a chance of getting healthy— and who pay."

Carl leaves, but his words continue to gnaw at me. He may sound heartless, but he's also a caring father and husband, and a committed doctor. And I know he's not uncharitable—he fund-raises for juvenile diabetes, a condition that affects his child.

The fact is, gerontology—the practice of medicine for the elderly—is one of the least popular specialties today. In 2005, there was only one geriatrician for every five thousand Americans sixty-five and older. Of one hundred forty-five medical schools in the United States, only nine have departments of geriatrics. A front page New York Times *article makes the point that medical students are drawn to sophisticated, expensive procedures— "laser this and endoscopic that"—which translate into more lucrative and prestigious careers. Most interventions for the elderly require creative, nonmedical solutions, like eliminating competing medications and promoting better diet and exercise. The goal is to manage, not cure, the patient. And that requires a lot of phone calls and hand-holding for a lot of unreimbursed time. Its reward? The gratitude*

of a helpless population and the highest job satisfaction
of any specialty, according to The Times, *a fact that may*
say as much about the individual who chooses geriatrics as
the specialty itself.

When I think of Carl, I both sympathize and identify
with him. In my practice, I'm seeing an elderly woman
who requires an inordinate amount of attention. She often
forgets appointments, and I don't have the heart to charge
her for missed time. She moves with glacial slowness, so I
schedule an extra half hour on either side of her appoint-
ment to walk her to and from her car. I spend as much time
coordinating her care with relatives and caretakers as I do
seeing her in my office. How would I feel having a whole
day's worth of these people? I don't know that I'd be so
generous.

REMEMBERING MOM
October 18, 2001

On a sparkling fall day, I take Dad to Apricot's, a restaurant
overlooking the Farmington River that serves organic salads
and burgers for lunch. It's a chance to have a tasty meal, enjoy
the brightly colored leaves, and hear the rush of the water.

I notice Dad staring at a couple, a man and woman, who
appear to be in their late sixties. Dad notices me noticing him
and says, "Look at them. They're lucky. They still have each
other."

I remember Dad telling me a few months after Mom died, "I reach out to her in bed and she's not there." I wonder, when he's silent, how much he thinks about her. Her name is so seldom on his lips.

Does he want to talk about Mom? Will I make him feel worse, tugging at his memories? Tugging at his heart?

Hesitantly, I ask, "Dad, do you know it's been about a year since Mom died?"

This man who can't remember where he put his watch down last night instantly shoots back, "October twenty-first—this Sunday."

The question, I realize, is not whether your parent remembers a deceased partner, but whether your parent remembers alone or with someone who cares enough to listen.

Money Secrets
December 26, 2001

My parents' attorney, Donna, advises Dad to give a chunk of cash to his family. "You're allowed to give each child and spouse ten thousand dollars a year without paying a gift tax," she explains.

"I don't understand," Dad says. "What if I need the money?"

"Your kids won't spend it. They'll invest it in their names, but if you need it, it's yours."

Dad looks rattled. "Are you telling me I have to leave Summerwood?" he asks.

Donna tells me later, "It's good financial planning to distribute forty thousand dollars of your father's money—ten thousand for each of you—but you don't have to stop there. You have power of attorney, so, if you're willing to pay the tax, why not transfer the bulk of his assets to you and Joel? If your father winds up in a nursing home, you only need to cover his expenses for three months—around thirty-six thousand dollars in Fairfield County—and then Medicaid takes over. Of course, the government's not going to let your father give all his money away the minute he gets sick, declare himself broke, and freeload off taxpayers the rest of his life, so the money must be off his name for three years before it's no longer considered his."

"It feels slimy, doing this behind his back."

"If he were less anxious and confused, he'd write the check himself. Your parents worked hard for their money. They'd want you and your brother to have it."

"Why should taxpayers subsidize my inheritance?"

"It's a tax loophole. Many families take advantage of them. They may be ethically questionable, but they're legal."

I decide to withdraw $40,000 and to provide Donna with copies of all my transactions. To make Dad feel more secure, I also give him an exact accounting of his savings, listing each asset, where it's invested, how much it's worth, and when it will mature. For example: Certificate of Deposit, Washington Mutual Bank, $18,234, maturing 12/3/02.

I bring him a copy. "Hi, Pop," I call out cheerfully as I enter his apartment. But I don't feel cheerful. I feel self-conscious, as though I'm smiling with a chipped tooth. Something strange and creepy has come between us. A secret.

"Hi, Sher," Dad responds warmly, adding to my guilt. His eyes are slightly watery but sharp. They seem to bore straight through me to the core of my deception.

I hand the report to Dad and watch him study it. I mean to be reassuring, to say, "See, you're fine financially. No reason to worry. I'm watching over you. You're in good hands."

But the report, of course, is bogus. The $40,000 I just distributed is not invested in Dad's name, as indicated, but in our names, and in banks not necessarily recorded on the statement. I made these gifts secretly, without his knowledge or consent.

"Can I keep this?" Dad asks.

"Sure," I answer, trying not to betray my guilt. "It's for you."

What's bothering me, what Donna hasn't prepared me for, is the impact of my deceit on my relationship with Dad. It's not just financial. It's visceral. And the change is immediate.

It may be okay to hide the truth from him since he can't understand it anyway, but suddenly I'm no longer a faithful friend and daughter, I'm a coconspirator with my brother, who knows and supports my strategy. I want desperately to tell Dad what I've done. I want his permission.

"Dad," I begin hesitantly, "I'm wondering how you're feeling about Donna's recommendation."

I pause. No response.

"About taking some money off your name, which Joel and I would hold in an account for you."

"I don't understand. Will the money be mine? What if I need it?"

I go over the plan again—our promise to invest his money and use it only for him, if he needs it. Dad stares out the window.

Oddly, on some level I feel betrayed by him. How could he not trust me? What makes him think I'd turn away from him, or against him? Since Mom died, I've done nothing but dedicate myself to him.

I welcome this flash of hurt and anger. It lightens my load of guilt and gives me a sanctimonious high. I could use the lift.

THE LOST WATCH
January 5, 2002

Seven-ten, Saturday morning. The phone rings. It's Pop.

"I can't find my watch," he declares. "The girl must have taken it. What's her number?"

I can hear the anxiety in his voice. The "girl" is Ann, his caretaker—the devoted nanny who comes in weekday mornings for an hour to get him up and running. She's a responsible, intelligent woman in her midthirties, with a warm olive complexion that rivals Halle Berry's. If Ann is dishonest, then Dad is a 007 agent.

Poor Dad, getting so worked up about a watch straight from a Delray Beach flea market with a faux-lizard band. It's an ailment endemic to the elderly—blaming others for their own absentmindedness. I suppose it's easier for Dad to fault a black aide from Jamaica than the real villain—old age.

What to do? He's visibly agitated, and I want to soothe him, but I can't validate his reality at Ann's expense. It's not fair to her. And we can't afford to lose her.

"Dad," I say gently, "I'm sure the watch is around. Maybe you could call Ann and ask her to help you find it."

I give him her number. At noon he calls back. "Jan, I've got a problem. I called what's-her-name. She said, 'Do you want me to come over?' I asked, 'Are you in the neighborhood?' 'No,' she said, 'but I'm happy to help.'"

Oy. An hour's drive on her day off.

Dad continues, "She walked in, went under my bed, and pulled out the watch. Just like that. How did she know it was there? Do you think she stole it?"

"Dad, is this your twelve-dollar watch or your good watch?"

A moment passes. "My five-dollar watch," he jokes.

"Pop, this is what happens when you get old. You think everyone is stealing from you. Ann has done nothing but nice things for you."

"I know," he admits. "I don't trust anyone anymore. So what do I say when I see her tomorrow? Do I ask her how come she knew where to look for the watch?"

"No, Pop. You thank her for coming over Saturday to help you."

"Okay," he replies, like a kid. "That's why I called. That's why you're a psychologist. I knew you'd have the answer. Good night." And he hangs up.

I take a deep breath and imagine what lies ahead for both of us. Is there any question that one day soon, I, too, will be on his list of offenders? That before long he won't realize that it's his mind, not his watch, that has been stolen?

PRUNES
January 19, 2002

Half a century ago, Izzy was a German immigrant supplying Singer sewing machines to Dad's fabric store. Today, at age ninety-two, his world is confined to Summerwood, where he joins us at the breakfast table with a bowl of stewed fruit. Beneath his black knit yarmulke is an elfin frame wrapped in layers, onion-like—a woolen sweater over a woolen vest over a plaid woolen shirt over a cotton undershirt.

I'm not the only one who notices him picking through the prunes.

"What are you doing?" asks Sam, wryly.

"Looking for one that's not wrinkled."

"Aren't we all?" Sam says.

He has a point. Whether we're searching for juicy fruit or juicy lives, we all prefer smooth to withered.

I'm reminded that under the word "old," my thesaurus offers two sets of synonyms. The first is unapologetically negative: archaic, bygone, crumbling, dated, decayed, moth-eaten, obsolete, outmoded, passé, unfashionable, worn-out. The second set offers a more positive view: constant, enduring, established, practiced, time-honored, skilled.

How do we learn to accentuate the positive? How do we go from "washed up" to "venerable," from "cast-off" to "vintage," from "outdated" to "experienced" and "wise"? I'm not optimistic we can. We live in a fast-paced, youth-obsessed society. As long as we value achievement over connection, outer beauty over inner beauty, and competence over kindness, the elderly will be mocked and marginalized, even by themselves.

HAROLD
February 22 and 29, 2002

When it comes to staying in touch with people, Dad gets low grades—from me, Joel, his grandkids, his friends. Even Harold.

Harold is Dad's one-time golf partner and closest friend. The two of them go back forty years to when they were members of Cliffside Country Club in Simsbury. Harold, a retired men's-clothing salesman, always dresses as though he's about to tee off. His signature outfit includes navy pin-striped seersucker pants, a canary yellow polo, and tassled loafers. Harold's heavy tortoiseshell glasses draw attention to his broad, hooked nose. The few wisps of hair he drags across his shiny scalp accentuate his baldness. His wife, at seventy-nine, still practices belly dancing, and line dances to country music. Mom never trusted her with Dad, so the two men would often get together without their wives.

Now that Dad is back in town, Harold calls him regularly. Almost every night, they watch sports together on television—baseball, football, golf—each in his own living room. Several times a year, Harold drives Dad to the Veteran's Home in Newington, a good thirty minutes away, where they get a physical and discounted medication. Harold can be a hypochondriac and a kvetch, but he's also a winning storyteller and very good company.

Dad never calls Harold. It's not that Dad isn't social; he loves to banter and has a genuine fondness for his buddy. Nor does Dad feel entitled to another person's friendship—he just doesn't initiate activity of any sort. People get hurt by this, reading it as a sign that they mean nothing to him, which isn't true.

Dad tells me, "Harold called and chewed me out last night."

"Oh yeah? What did he say?"

"He said, 'You never call me. That's not nice!' I told him, 'Harold, it's not like I lead an exciting life. It's not like I have anything to report about.' You know what Harold said? 'But things go on in *my* life. Today I went to the doctor!'"

"Well, Pop, I'm sure Harold would like you to reach out to him once in a while."

"Yeah. But Harold goes to the doctor every day."

A week passes, and Dad brings me up to date. "Sher, you'd be proud of me. I called Harold today. 'This is your friend Louie,' I said. 'I'm not calling you to tell you anything. I'm not calling to bother you for anything. I'm just calling to see how you are.'"

"What did Harold say?"

"He told me, 'That's very good.' "

Who says old dogs can't learn new tricks?

To Be of Use
April 8, 2002

When Mom was alive, she ran the show and Dad never lifted a finger, not even to make coffee. The more children do for their aging parents, the more helpless they become, so when Dad moved into Summerwood, I deliberately assigned him some chores to encourage his independence.

Every week, Summerwood vacuums and dusts Dad's apartment, and changes his linens. But he's responsible for washing his own clothes. I could ask his aide to help, but he should tackle this task on his own. What else does he have to do with his time? Besides, it will force him out of his chair and get his blood pumping.

Dad doesn't embrace the job with much enthusiasm, but he doesn't complain either. Occasionally, I get a call, "How many minutes do I set the dryer for?" or "How much powder do I put in?" When I visit, I see the mistakes—polo shirts dried to death, lost socks, a pile of wet clothes sitting in the washroom unclaimed. But, for the most part, he's rising to the challenge.

Other residents are, too, and not just the men. Yesterday, Dad found a bra in the dryer with his undershirts. He niddle-noddled down the hallway, holding up the goods, until he found the owner.

In addition to doing his laundry, Dad waters the Kentia palm in his living room. It's thriving, and Dad seems to take pride in its growth, even though I have to remind him to give it a drink once in a while.

It's important for everyone, old and young, to keep themselves busy with meaningful work, to develop an I-can-manage sense of themselves in order to maintain their self-respect and autonomy. Pampering them, making life easier for them, isn't doing them a favor—it's only reinforcing their sense of irrelevance. Babying Dad would only turn him into a baby—and that's too easy, both for him and for me.

I believe this categorically, even as I head for the washroom to give his new polo shirt a rinse.

WHY I VISIT DAD
May 30, 2002

Why do I visit Dad? What motivates me?

Love, of course. Love manifests itself not just in how we feel toward someone, but in how we treat them.

Is it guilt? I'd feel crummy about myself, ignoring the person who has nurtured me for fifty-five years. How great is my debt?

Is it compassion? Dad is nearing the end of his life and can't manage by himself. It must be hard to be so dependent, so fragile, so alone.

Is it to relieve my anxiety? Taking control of his life, I feel more in control of my own. When I'm in charge, I worry less about how he's doing because I know he's getting the attention he needs.

What about pleasure? No question, all the tender moments we have shared have sweetened my life.

Here's a reason I visit Dad that I was unaware of when I started this journey, but am sure of today—it makes me feel like a decent human being. Thoreau said, "Aim above morality. Be not simply good, be good for something." When I make what's left of his life happier and more comfortable, I feel grounded and good about myself.

And another reason: when I visit, I'm touched by the humanity, the courage that he and the other elderly residents display daily. I walk into Summerwood and see Sarah, ninety years old, sitting in the lounge, reading the newspaper. Why does she bother? Will she remember the headlines by dinnertime? Her goals may be more modest, less noble than those of presidents and policy makers, but they're no less important. She reads to keep her mind alive. She makes the best of the time she has left. She hasn't given up or written herself off. I admire her grasp on life and am moved and inspired by her determination.

One more reason—I'm reminded that these people are me, if I'm so lucky to live as long and as well as they do. Their journey foreshadows mine. I'm next, coming down the pike faster than the seasons change from green to white.

I also visit so my kids will visit me someday. I set a model I hope they'll follow when I'm strapped to a wheelchair in the lobby of a nursing home, dying for their tender touch.

Generations

My patient Sybil comes to see me after a year's absence, looking thinner and more drawn. "It kills me, how my daughter treats my father," she tells me. "Alice is twenty-one, she should know better. Dad's ninety-two with esophageal cancer. The chemo's not working and his hands are swollen like sausages, but he tries so hard to be a good sport and not complain. My heart goes out to him."

Sybil shakes her head. "The other day Alice told me she was driving to Boston to see a friend. I pleaded with her, 'Stop in Worcester to see your grandpa. He's five minutes off the highway.' So what does she do? She gets off at Dad's exit and pulls into a Dairy Queen for a waffle-cone sundae. No call. No visit. Believe me, this kid's life is a cakewalk—what would it cost her to spend five minutes with her grandfather? She has to know how much it would mean to him. And to me. I'm ashamed of her selfishness. I'm ashamed of myself, raising a kid with such screwed-up values. I can just imagine, when I get older, how she's going to treat me."

"It hurts, doesn't it," I acknowledge. "We do so much for our kids and then they let us down and we feel betrayed. But we compound our misery when we think we're the only ones whose kids disappoint us. I hear your story every day—from good parents talking about their basically good kids. You're not alone: 'To be a parent is to know the meaning of failure.' But tell me, weren't there times, as a child, when you were just as unfeeling, just as selfish as your daughter?"

Sybil runs her hands through a thick mane of peppery hair. "When I was in college, my father had open-heart surgery and developed an infection. He was in the hospital for a month. I was off doing my own thing. I don't remember ever visiting him. It blows my mind."

"You need to be young to be so oblivious. Alice is still a kid—she thinks she'll live forever. What does she know about sickness and dying? All you can do is try to judge her fairly and not demonize her. And set a good example."

Sybil wipes an eye, leaving a dark smudge. "Well," she concedes, "the truth is, she's a good person, though too *self-absorbed for my taste. Last month she called Dad on his birthday and made him laugh. As for setting an example, I pray what I do for Dad rubs off on her. If she gives me half the attention I've given him, I'll be lucky."*

I smile weakly. *"We look after our parents out of guilt, sympathy, and love, but also out of fear—fear that when we reach their age, our kids will pass us up for something sweeter and easier to swallow . . . like a waffle-cone sundae."*

PEOPLE SKILLS
June 19, 2002

With time to spare, Dad and I spend the morning checking out a new independent-living facility in town. It's more posh than Summerwood, with a heated indoor pool and a full-time gerontologist, but it's too formal for Dad's taste, and too sprawling for a man with his disabilities. Before long, his arthritic hip begins to throb, so I park him in the lobby and finish the tour without him. When I return, he's chatting with a resident. The man must be pushing ninety. "My name's Benjamin," he says, offering me his huge, leathery hand. "But you can call me Jaime."

"Hi, Jaime. How long have you been here?"

"Since it opened."

Dad jumps in, "Have they made you president yet?"

Jaime grins back. "Not even mayor."

If Dad lived here, I'm sure these two would be buddies. Sam tells me Dad could be mayor of Summerwood, he makes friends so easily. But Dad isn't running for office. He has no agenda, no need to impress or win anyone over.

Later that day, waiting on line at the pharmacy, Dad remarks to the dour woman beside him, "I like your red coat." She immediately perks up. "I have two!"

A minute ago, she and Dad were strangers. Now the two of them share a chuckle, momentarily forgetting the ailments that have brought them together.

On the way out, Dad runs into Helen, an old family friend, recently widowed. Dad, stooped over from osteoporosis, lifts his head and observes: "Your hair looks nice. You must have just come from the beauty parlor."

Helen lights up. "You're right!" she says, glowing like a young girl.

If Dad were a ladies' man, he would be a killer, luring victims with a few choice words and a smile. But Dad is just being who he is, making people feel good about themselves, making them feel they matter.

Some people use language as a weapon to put others down or build themselves up. Dad uses it like a feather, tickling them with humor, making them laugh and relax. I'm learning how important this asset is when you're old and alone. It's then that your achievements no longer give you a leg up in the world, and who you're related to matters less than how you relate. At Dad's age, it's not your money, it's your ability to get along, your social grace, that makes you rich.

Dad never went to college, but he could teach a course in

people skills. As I watch him feel his way, with no one to lean on or take his hand, I wonder if I'll do as well when my turn comes. Right now, I'm Dad's caretaker. But he's still my mentor. "Healthy children will not fear life," Erik Erikson wrote, "if their elders have integrity enough not to fear death."

SOPHIE
July 8, 2002

I walk into Dad's apartment and find him sunk deep in his green recliner, watching the morning news.

"The poppa! The poppa!" I sing.

"Hi, Sher."

We head downstairs for breakfast. Sam and Murray have eaten and left by now, so we choose an empty table, fill up our plates at the buffet, and settle down to some catch-up conversation. I relish these times with Dad.

I'm smearing his bagel with cream cheese when Sophie, an eighty-eight-year-old Russian immigrant, waddles over to our table.

"What are you doing today, Sophie?" I ask, trying to be friendly. Dad flashes me a look that says, "That's a mistake." I quickly learn why.

"I'm going to the Crown Market at ten," Sophie says, vacantly. Then she pulls out her grocery list and takes us through it, item by item. "I buy cucumbers for cucumber salad. I like their salami. Some milk . . ."

I try to cut her off. "We're heading out to do errands, too."

She keeps talking, oblivious to my cue. "My son's a dentist. He comes here to visit me twice a week. . . ."

"Sophie," Dad says, respectfully, but more firmly than usual. "This is my daughter. She's here just for a couple of hours. We're having breakfast. We don't want to hear about your son, the dentist."

"Oh," Sophie says, unfazed.

As she drifts off toward another table, the other residents lower their heads, study their eggs, resisting her interest in engaging them. I'm stunned by her intrusiveness, her insensitivity to how people experience her. There must be something wrong with her, perhaps a neurological or psychiatric problem like Asperger's syndrome. She seems to lack the compensatory skills necessary to relate to others in socially acceptable ways.

Outside, Dad whispers jokingly, "She's the biggest pain in the ass. Do you know how many times I've heard about her son the dentist?"

As we head back upstairs, I find myself wondering how much of our behavior is due to disease or aging, and how much captures exactly who we are, who we've always been. Yes, life can make us tactless and self-absorbed, but some of us never change, whatever happens. The ones who are sweet-tempered in their youth often remain affable and good-natured as they ripen. You can pick them out at Summerwood; they're a pleasure to be around. The annoying ones probably elicit the same reaction they elicited as kids. Someone like Sophie probably doesn't understand the way she provokes her own isolation. I feel for her—but I also feel for Dad.

One of the hazards of living in a communal setting like Summerwood is that when you leave your room you're no longer in your private domain and will bump into people like Sophie, whether you like it or not. To last here, you have to set limits on the amount of compassion you dole out to others, and switch into self-protective gear from time to time.

Dad and I retreat into his apartment and close the door securely behind us.

CHOICES
September 10, 2002

My mother's youngest sister, Babe, has just been diagnosed with liver cancer. Her kids, my first cousins, have scheduled appointments for her with expert oncologists at both Sloan-Kettering and their local hospital. Their intervention fans my guilt and makes me question how I'm managing my father's health. I know he has a mysterious spot on his liver that has shown up on CAT scans, but his doctor suggests I let it go unless I'm planning to put him through rigorous tests and perhaps chemotherapy or surgery. I decide to take his advice and not act.

There's another part of me, however, that wonders, "Who am I to cast this vote? Am I betraying my father? Some day my kids may need to make similar God-like decisions about my care—will they convince themselves that I'm so over the hill, so past my prime, that another month or year doesn't matter?

The power to make health-care decisions for another human being is daunting, more than we deserve, more than we want, more than we signed up for.

THE DRIVING TEST
October 18–19, 2002

Dad is still driving, God help us, and wants to renew his license in the state of Connecticut. Does this make sense? His reflexes are slow, his mind is fuzzy, and his head hangs so low on his chest, he can barely see over the dashboard. Yet he doesn't drive fast and he doesn't drive far—no farther than the Crown Market to buy a Hershey bar, or the local mall to catch a matinee. I'm not brave enough or sure enough to deprive him of this privilege, so I drive him to the Department of Motor Vehicles to let him prove himself.

Time crawls. When we finally emerge from the line, we're told we need two forms of identification.

Dad fumbles with his wallet and pulls out a battered card from the U.S. Army, verifying his honorary discharge in 1944.

"Sorry," the clerk says. "This is a copy. We need the original."

"You've got to be joking," I protest. "My dad's a vet. Can't you give him a break?"

"A rule's a rule. We're open most days eight to four. Next."

Dad and I head back home, worn out and dejected. The next day I search my safe-deposit box and, among Mom's papers, find Dad's social security card and an original copy of his service papers. Bingo.

Back at the Motor Vehicles department, Dad peers at a screen as the examiner, a man close to him in years, tests his sense of perspective. "Which block is closest to you?" he asks. "The red, the blue, or the green?"

Dad guesses—wrong. The examiner gives him another stab. Dad misses again.

The inquisition goes on. "Well," the examiner says, "your depth perception is terrible, but you don't need to pass that part to get a license."

Dad nods approvingly. The man studies him. "Do me a favor," he says. "Don't drive unless you have to, and look over your shoulder before changing lanes."

Dad couldn't turn his head if his life depended on it, but he smiles in agreement. So do I.

The man then proclaims, music to Dad's ears: "I waive all further tests and pass you."

Dad sticks out his paw. "You're a gentleman," he says, grinning with gratitude.

Gentleman or not, the man has chosen to give Dad a gift—not only a renewed license, but a renewed lease on life, at least for today. I agonize over the idea of letting him drive, risking lives, including his own, but I go along for the ride. Call me reckless, irresponsible, or cowardly, I join a long line of children who don't have the heart to take away a parent's keys.

AN APPLE FOR RUTH
December 8, 2002

Dave's Parkinson's is advancing, but any day he can, he hops on the Summerwood van and takes it a mile down the road to the Hebrew Home and Hospital to visit his wife, Ruth. There she lies, detached from the world, suffering her own disgrace from Alzheimer's—if she only knew. The fact that she no longer recognizes him, doesn't, in his mind, diminish the importance of his mission.

Dave's commitment reminds me of a story Rabbi Israel Stein told at a Yom Kippur service:

A man sits in a doctor's office, waiting to be seen. The doctor is running late. The man walks over to the front desk and tells the receptionist he needs to leave; he has an appointment. "Every day," he explains, "I have lunch with my wife at twelve-thirty. She's in a nursing home with Alzheimer's."

"So does she know you?" the nurse asks.

"No."

"So she must not know what time of day you come."

"True."

"So why is it so important that you're there?"

"Because even though she doesn't know who *I* am, I haven't forgotten who *she* is."

It's Dad's eighty-third birthday today, and I've invited his buddies to gather in his apartment at six to go out for dinner. Sam and Murray arrive promptly, one toting a bottle of Merlot, the other, a supersize Hershey bar. Dave comes ten minutes later, looking flustered.

"I apologize for being late," he says. "It took me twenty minutes to put on these socks." He lifts the leg of his pants and shows off his efforts. "There has to be an easier way."

Dad chuckles sympathetically.

The men mosey down to the car. We pick up Helen, then head over to the Butterfly restaurant for a Chinese feast.

"There's nothing like a little *traife* for dinner," Dad chimes in. *Traife* is Yiddish for nonkosher food—shrimp, lobster, pork—which is strictly forbidden at Summerwood.

Dave, whose temperament is usually upbeat and playful, seems particularly quiet and depressed tonight.

"How are you?" I ask.

"I wasn't able to visit Ruth today," he tells me, sorrowfully. "My aide took the day off, and Summerwood wouldn't allow me on the van without her."

The authorities rule, and they're not wrong—Dave is too wobbly to walk unassisted. I'm nervous just ushering him from the parking lot to the restaurant. Dave, nonetheless, has the right to register his complaint. There are so many losses these men must contend with: not only the loss of their life partners, but the loss of their health and freedom of movement. In his youth, Dave was a respected community leader with advanced degrees, who served on boards of banks and private schools. Today, he's reduced to a dependent cripple, fumbling with his socks, pleading for permission to visit his ailing wife who has forgotten his name.

"How is she doing?" I ask.

"She's eating less and less," he replies sadly.

But then he perks up and says, "Yesterday, your dad gave me a Macoun apple to give her. I told her it was from Lou, and she grabbed it and took a bite." He smiles at Dad, who smiles back.

We sit down for dinner and for the next hour and a half pig out on spareribs, deep-fried dumplings, pork egg rolls. Several times Dave gets quiet and seems to slip into depression. Each time, Dad leans over and quips to him, "So, she took the apple!" And Dave immediately brightens and says, "Can you imagine? I didn't think she had the strength."

We finish up with bowls of coconut ice cream and cups of green tea. As I help the group take trips to the bathroom and put on their coats, Dave whispers to me: "Ruth did eat the apple—the whole thing. But I'm sorry to say, I don't think she understood when I said, 'It's from Lou.' "

THE DREAM
February 18–21, 2003

Five p.m. I call Dad promptly, knowing this is a good time to find him refreshed from an afternoon nap. I imagine him settled in his easy chair with a glass of Merlot, maybe some nuts or cheese and crackers, watching the news until Sam comes by to accompany him to dinner.

"Hi," Dad grunts into the phone. I wait for him to follow up with a question, some playful banter, but he's uncharacteristically quiet.

"Are you okay?"

"Yeah." In the background, I hear a woman's voice, laughing, chattering away.

"Who's there?" I ask innocently.

"No one."

"Please say hello to your daughter for me," I hear a voice call out. It sounds like Evelyn Bernstein, a woman who has made her affection for Dad clear.

I'm confused. "Is that Evelyn? Is Evelyn there?" I ask.

"No," he says adamantly.

How peculiar. If I had caught him watching porn or smoking a joint, he wouldn't sound more awkward or self-conscious.

The next day, Dad confesses the truth. Before Evelyn's husband passed away, the couple shared a cocktail in their apartment every night before dinner—Summerwood only serves alcohol, a glass of kosher wine, on Shabbat. Dad told Evelyn he pours himself a drink around five, and she asked if she could join him. His reply was vintage Dad: "Why not?"

I'm sure that's exactly how it happened. And I'm sure that when she took his cue, he was both delighted and uneasy.

I step in to register my approval. "That's great, Dad. Evelyn is very good company. I worry about you spending too much time alone."

Another day passes. Dad calls me around two. This is unusual. Something is on his mind.

"Hi," he says.

"Hi, Pop. What's up?"

"I had a dream."

"Really? Do you want to tell me about it?"

"Will you charge me?" Dad tries to joke, but I can hear he's agitated.

"Your mother and I were dating," he recounts. "We weren't married yet. She told me Saul Friedman asked her out—and she didn't know what to say." Dad stops to reflect on this and gather strength. "I was terribly upset. I thought he was my best friend. Why didn't she say no to this guy?"

"What are you thinking?" I ask.

"I'm wondering, why am I dreaming this? Was she interested in him? Did they have something going on between them?"

I never knew my mother to be disloyal to Dad. Not even in her dreams. She had a brief flirtation with a man from our synagogue, but that was before Dad came along. Years later, during the High Holy Days, she pointed him out in the sanctuary and told me, "You see that man? I dated him before I met your father." I used to stare at him and try to imagine him kissing Mom.

Dad wasn't the disloyal type either, although when I was really young, maybe five, he and Mom had a major blowup and she accused him of being too friendly with a woman at a neighbor's party. She packed her suitcase and marched out of the house. I ran after her, begging her to come home. I don't remember what happened after that, except that they made up, and Mom told me she wasn't going to put up with his wandering eye again.

Dad's nightmare? I have no idea what it's about. Even if I were trained in dream analysis, which I'm not, my only goal would be to help him make sense of it so he could put it to rest and perhaps benefit from it.

"Dad," I say, "I don't know what your dream means, but it's the meaning *you* give it that upsets you."

"You think I'm making it up?"

"No. But it's possible"—and here I proceed more cautiously—"that your dream isn't about Mom at all, but about you. Sometimes in our dreams we switch characters around."

I pause, then try to make my point diplomatically. "Maybe you feel guilty for having a drink with Evelyn?"

"I don't feel guilty," Dad retorts.

"Well, maybe you don't *know* that you feel guilty but unconsciously you do."

"I really don't feel guilty," Dad insists.

The next day Dad calls again and blurts out, "Sher, I really *do* feel bad for inviting her into my apartment."

"Well," I respond reassuringly, "I think it's great to invite a friend over. Why be alone when you can enjoy someone's company? It doesn't mean you love Mom any less if you make new friends."

It feels weird, giving Dad permission to socialize with other women. I'm sure Mom wouldn't like it. I'm sure she'd see *me* as disloyal, an accomplice to a crime, for liking Evelyn and encouraging Dad to make new connections. This may be terribly unfair to say, but I suspect she'd rather Dad be lonely than be with another woman, even now, two and a half years after her death. Dad clearly feels disloyal to her, his soul mate for half a century.

So how should Dad think about dating in this last chapter of his life? Some people might assume that if a widower gets attached to another woman, he must not have loved his wife that much. Others might argue the opposite—that if he gets attached to someone else, it's *because* he loved his wife, had a good marriage, and wants to repeat the experience. New love can be a tribute to old love. Or not. There's no absolute truth here.

Meanwhile, I watch Dad's conflicted journey from widower to bachelor. The steps he is taking are wrenching, guilt-inducing, and, someday, I hope, intoxicating.

LOCKED IN THE CAR
April 30, 2003

"I'm losing my marbles," Dad announces, looking visibly shaken.

"What happened?"

"You're not going to believe it."

Trust me. Nothing will surprise me. "Go ahead," I say, bracing myself for the worst.

"Last night, Helen came for dinner. Sam's sister picked her up and brought her to Summerwood, and the four of us ate in the dining room. Then I drove her home."

I state the obvious: "Dad, you shouldn't be driving at night."

"Well, you're not going to believe what happened. I got back home, and I couldn't get out of the car."

"You couldn't lift yourself off the seat?"

Dad recounts the nightmare, his face flush with embarrassment: "I was in the parking lot, alone. It was dark. I couldn't figure out how to open the door. I was trapped inside, and panicked. I didn't know how to get out."

"How terrible," I commiserate.

"Finally, someone saw me and opened the door."

"Was it locked?"

"No. I forgot how to get out. Can you believe it?"

Yes, unfortunately, I can. How frightening it must be when you can't perform a simple task you've done your whole life. It's hard enough to look at something and not know what it's called, but imagine not knowing what it is, how it works, what it's used for. Imagine yourself standing helplessly by, watching the slow unclenching of your mind.

Too Tired to Bother
June 15, 2003

Father's Day. The family sits on the screened-in porch at Sister Sue's, the air scented with lilac.

Dad is the picture of contentment, propped up in a cushioned armchair, pulled close to the table. Most of the conversation revolves around others, but his presence is acknowledged as we offer him second helpings, refill his glass, and jump up to mop his clothes as he navigates the food to his lips.

The afternoon is spent, and so are we. Dad is zipped into his beige Bobby Jones polyester jacket and heading for the car, when he asks to use the toilet. I leave him at the bathroom door and stand by in case he falls.

I hear the faltering stream, then the muffled words: "Jan, come see."

I push my way inside. The bowl is filled with bloody urine. Dad has peed blood before, but it has always cleared up in a day or two. His urologist has told me not to worry, it can happen to someone like Dad with a history of prostate and bladder cancers. It's Sunday—should I call the doctor? I could take him to the hospital, but do I really want to spend the night in an emergency room? I'm exhausted.

Michael and I bring Dad back to Summerwood. He's not complaining, so we hug him good-bye and head for the highway. It's hard to know when a problem is serious and when it's not. And sometimes you just can't deal with problems anymore, no matter how serious they are.

A GREAT BAGEL
July 25, 2003

Dad and I pay a visit to his eighty-five-year-old friend Arthur Levy, who was struck down by Alzheimer's and a stroke, and is living, if you can call it that, in the Hebrew Home and Hospital.

Dad can't walk far these days, so I sit him in a wheelchair and push him into the facility, first stopping at the front desk to ask for Arthur's room number. "He's on the second floor," the receptionist tells me. *Oh, no.* The Hebrew Home is like a filing cabinet. If you're on the first floor, you're in rehab and recovery is possible. On the second, you're filed away for life. The only way out is through the basement, the morgue.

Dad and I get into the elevator and push "2." We find Arthur fastened to a wheelchair, in front of a blaring TV, slumped to one side. "Hi, Art," Dad calls out. Arthur doesn't respond. His gaze is fixed on something far away. "Hi, Art," Dad says again. I try to intervene in a perky voice. "Arthur, Louie Lieff has come to visit you. How are you?"

Arthur looks at Dad as though he's seeing him for the first time. He registers nothing. "Let's go," Dad says. He shakes his head, noticeably disturbed, and mutters under his breath, "terrible," and again, "terrible."

The two of us are relieved to get back into the car and head to a fresh fruit stand on a back country road. Dad is subdued, even more so than usual. I get the feeling that he'd rather die than be like Arthur—so vacant, so stripped of functioning.

We stuff a bag full of Washington cherries, bursting with color and flavor, and drive to an outdoor café in West Hartford Center. Dad's favorite table is waiting for us, right along the sidewalk, where he can eat a hearty brunch and eye the young, trendy shoppers parading by. He has his agenda, I have mine—to probe his thoughts on dying.

Death is no stranger to Dad. He has lost two generations of loved ones and must know, given his list of ailments, that he's a medical miracle to have survived them all. With Arthur still on our minds, I speak the unspeakable. My approach is gentle but hardly indirect.

"Dad, may I ask, do you ever think about dying?"

About three seconds pass before he answers flatly, "No."

I try to keep the subject on the table, just in case he wants to say more. "I think about it all the time," I say.

Another few seconds pass, then, with a wicked twinkle in his eye, he announces, "Isn't this a great bagel?"

The truth is, it *is* a great bagel. And what makes it even greater is that it's smeared with real vegetable cream cheese— not the low-fat, doctor-prescribed kind, but the big, buttery, loaded-with-cholesterol kind. And the coffee is smacking-hot and delicious. And we're sitting outdoors, not in a home for the elderly, and Dad can still pick up that monster and stuff it into his face with his own two hands. *So, why, why talk about dying now?* I take the cue, sit back, and let the sun warm the space between us.

AN ACT OF KINDNESS
September 1, 2003

While visiting Dad, I come across a handwritten note on his dining-room table. It reads,

> *Dear Louie,*
> *I will always remember how supportive and caring you were when I came to Summerwood. I was feeling very sad and lost in my new surroundings. Good health and good feelings to a mensch.*
> *Many thanks,*
> *Marion T.*

"What's this?" I ask.

Dad explains.

Last winter, a woman named Marion and her husband, Sidney, flew from Florida to West Hartford to visit their son. During their stay, Sidney slipped on the bathroom floor and broke his leg, and was forced to spend a month in rehab at the Hebrew Home. Marion checked into Summerwood alone.

One day, Dad came down for breakfast and saw her sitting at a table, crying, all alone. He sat down beside her and said, "It can't be that bad. Let's talk it over."

She told him her story and they became friends. "I can't believe you're so nice to me," she would say. "I can't believe you're so nice to me."

Eventually, her husband got better, the couple went back to Florida, and she sent Dad this note.

"She's a nice lady," Dad says.

What happened between Marion and Dad at Summerwood? I imagine that during her stay, Dad ran into her and asked, "How's Sidney?" and Marion lit up, so appreciative of having someone break through her loneliness and anxiety, and care about her pain. I picture her saying, "He's doing better, Lou," and Dad replying, "That's good," and smiling at her. I'm sure what happened most was that Marion talked and Dad listened.

I ask Dad if he'd like to write back to Marion. "I can't," he laments. "My hands shake terribly." So, I compose a brief note saying how nice it is to hear from her and how pleased Dad is that Sidney is feeling better. I hand a pen over to Dad to sign his name. He hands it back. I return it to him with a glance that says, "No, it will be better if you do it, no matter how it looks." He scribbles "Lou," which I translate into block letters below his signature. I add my own, and mail the letter.

Another couple of weeks pass, and Marion follows up with a second note, which I find in Dad's stack of mail:

Dear Louie,

I'm thinking of you and hope all is well and that you're enjoying good health. I miss your warm presence and gentle manner. Warmest regards to your daughter.

Fondly,

Marion

I doubt Dad would have told me about their friendship if I hadn't found the notes. My first thought is, maybe Dad could marry Marion someday. Dad needs a Marion, and Marion needs someone like Dad. But then there's her husband, Sidney, which makes it complicated.

My second, more circumspect thought is that what happened between Dad and Marion is nothing more complicated than an act of human kindness—one person pouring out her pain, another listening with compassion. Nothing fancy or profound.

Dad is a mensch, and he's a great listener. So many times I've been in Marion's shoes, talking out my troubles to him. He hears me out attentively, without judgment—often, without comment.

Listening is a powerful act of healing. At any age. Psychologist Judith Jordan makes the point: *We listen one another into being.*

THE PEE BOTTLE
October 20–24, 2003

Last week Dad tripped on his way to the bathroom in the middle of the night and fractured his collarbone. How many more falls can the man survive?

"So, Dad," I explain, in a casual, no-big-deal tone of voice, "when you hit the floor, you were half drunk on sleep. If you had stayed in bed, you would have saved yourself a lot of trouble."

Dad gives me a look that says, "I'm with you so far."

"So, what if you try to pee in a bottle, sitting up in bed?"

"Like in the hospital," Dad replies.

"Right. But at home."

"Okay. That's easy."

But, of course, nothing is easy with Dad. He has trouble just hoisting himself up, never mind slipping his penis into a urinal with his arm in a sling.

Days go by. When I return to Dad's apartment, I find his aide squatting on the bedroom floor, sorting and folding a mountain of laundry.

"Is he using the urinal?" I ask.

"He's trying to. But he pees on everything—the blanket, the carpet, his pajamas. His whole body stinks."

The day is young, sunlight radiates through the apartment, and Dad is wide-awake. As the aide leaves, I turn to him and suggest a dry run, as it were.

"Hey, Pop, how about we practice peeing in the bottle?"

"Sure."

"Okay. Let's try it. Lie down."

Dad lumbers over to the bed and plops down. He struggles to raise his legs up on the mattress, and ends up precariously close to the edge, feet dangling off the side. *How many times have I shown him how to do this?*

He starts fumbling with his fly. I step outside and busy myself in the kitchenette.

"Okay," I call out, "all systems go."

"Close the door," he chuckles.

I follow his orders, and wait. And wait. Dad finally emerges, shuffles over to the bathroom, and closes the door behind him. I peer into his room. The pee bottle sits empty on his bed.

I bristle at Dad for not trying harder. Surely he knows he's risking another fall, and leaving me to pick up the pieces. I'm the one, after all, who has to place him in rehab, organize his caregivers, deal with doctors and Medicare. He's not just hurting himself, he's hurting me.

But another part of me knows I'm stirring up my own trouble. Why do I assume Dad is going to change? How stupid is that? How silly the way we, the children, keep trying to remake our parents, and mold them to our wills. Why are we put out when they refuse to be anyone but themselves? *When will we learn: old dogs sometimes don't learn new tricks.*

A GOOD POOP
November 12, 2003

"I'm terribly constipated," Dad reports. Probably a side effect of Vicodin, pain medication he's taking for his fracture.

"Do you have any milk of magnesia?" I ask.

"No. I've never taken a laxative in my life. Your mother took them every night."

Boy, do I remember that. Mom seemed to spend half her life in the bathroom, battling constipation. And could I have been any more unsympathetic? Yet here I am, micromanaging Dad's bowels.

I call at night for a progress report.

"Hi, Pop. How are you?"

"Terrific!" he declares with conviction.

"Terrific?" What could be so terrific?

"The nurse ordered something from the pharmacy, and I took a capful. Then around dinner I had to go so badly, I barely made it to the toilet."

"Nothing like a good poop," I acknowledge cheerfully.

Now there's a fine definition of love: when you're as happy about someone else's poop as you are about your own.

It's My Turn
February 3, 2004

Today I begin the tour for my second book, *How Can I Forgive You? The Courage to Forgive, The Freedom Not To.* My first stop: Washington, D.C. I plan to catch the train at two, check into a boutique hotel near the capital, and get a good night's sleep before the challenges of tomorrow. Harper-Collins has set up two great kickoff venues for me—The Smithsonian Institute and *The Diane Rehm Show* on NPR.

I call Dad early, just to check in.

"I'm in bed," he croaks. "My hip is killing me. I can't walk."

My heart sinks. This is unreal. Whom can I call to help? Michael is at a sales conference. My brother and sister-in-law have already left for work. Managing this crisis is more than I can ask of anyone, even Sister Sue.

I'm so angry at myself I could scream. I've known about my book tour for a year. Why didn't I protect myself from this kind of scramble?

Why? Because full-time help costs a fortune. Because most reliable part-time aides aren't available at a moment's notice. Because there are health decisions that must be made and only I can make them.

"I'm on my way," I assure him. I say nothing about the book tour, nothing about myself. It's eighty minutes to Summerwood, then two hours to deal with Dad, eighty minutes back home, thirty minutes to the train. . . . I can still make it.

I call Dad's doctor from the car. He tells me to bring him to the radiology lab on Jefferson Street for a hip X-ray.

"Sure," I say, "no problem."

Somehow, Dad gets his tests and I make my train. Dad's hip isn't broken. His pain is probably arthritic, which is uncomfortable but not life-threatening. I call a home-care worker I've used before and arrange for her to move in with him until I return.

"Give Dad extra-strength Tylenol whenever he needs it," is the best over-the-counter advice I can give.

Sitting on the train, rattling through a white, wintry world, I'm happy Dad's problem is under control. I'm also happy—ecstatic—to be relieved of my responsibility for him, to be rid of him, for two full days. Getting out of town, turning my attention to myself and the book I've spent the last three years writing, I can hardly contain my excitement.

Ingratitude

"My mother never says thank you," a patient named Margaret complains. "I visit her religiously in the nursing home. My brother—where is he? He only lives a few miles away, but he never stops by. On Mother's Day, I

brought her a batch of toffee-chip cookies and some fun,
faux-pearl earrings. I washed and dyed her hair. It would
be nice if she acknowledged that I'm a good daughter. It
hurts me that she doesn't."

How often do I hear this: the lament of the caring
child, saddled with a parent who is cranky, entitled,
fault-finding, and self-absorbed?

"Your frustration and anger make sense," I tell Mar-
garet, "given how nasty your mother has been. It's hard
to sacrifice for someone who takes you for granted—as
hard as it is to forgive someone who doesn't show remorse
for making you suffer. But you hurt yourself, getting so
riled up, so derailed, every time she lets you down. A pa-
tient named Carol once told me, 'Every time I buy my
mother a gift, she returns it. I buy her a pocketbook, she
returns it. I buy her a nightgown, she returns it.' I told
her, 'Carol, if you want to buy your mother a present,
that's fine. But at some point you have to stop being sur-
prised or upset when she takes it back.' I'd say the same to
you. Your mother is ninety-one. By now, she is who she is.
Your emotional health hinges on your ability to stop in-
sisting that she change, and work on changing the way
you think about her.

"For starters, it would help if you could take her
moodiness less personally. It's not that she became short-
tempered and high-strung overnight, she's been that way
her whole life, and not just toward you. It's possible she
was born with a chemical imbalance or genetic anomaly
that makes her bristly and contentious. Or she could have

learned her behavior from her rageful father, who gave her too little and left her starved for more. She could still be jealous of the attention your father showered on you. Who knows why she's so difficult. There are a thousand possible explanations, and most of them probably have less to do with you than you think.

"You could blame old age and sickness, too. Your mother has gotten more irascible over time, screaming at you, making constant demands. Maybe she's unable to get beyond her pain. Maybe she's losing her mind, literally, and doesn't realize how sharp she sounds.

"And here's something else to consider: however difficult it is for you to care for an ungrateful mother, it's harder for her to admit her dependence on you. The more she needs you, the more she may resent you. There's an old Yiddish proverb: when parents feed their children, they both laugh; when children feed their parents, they both cry.

"In the end, your mother may not deserve your love. You choose to care for her not because of who she is, but because of who you are. Because you couldn't live with yourself otherwise. And so you trudge on and indulge her, never giving up the hope that someday, before she dies, she'll notice, and say thank you."

VALENTINE'S DAY
February 14, 2004

It's Valentine's Day. Summerwood serves up heart-shaped candies and gathers the residents for a party.

Jean, the recreational director, asks the group, "Would anyone like to share a love story?" A small, feisty resident named Sarah jumps up and talks about her deceased husband—how much she loved him, and how annoying he was. Ed, who's ninety-two, is next. He came to Summerwood when his wife died two years ago and started dating Mildred, who is also widowed. "I just want all of you to know that Mildred and I are very happy," he proclaims, "and we're planning to move in together and get married."

Everyone claps and cheers and heads for the refreshments. Dad is all grins. It's the perfect time to tell him that his grandson Aaron may be getting engaged. "He's talking about buying Ali a ring," I announce.

"No kidding," Dad says, approvingly. Then he brings the conversation home. "I remember when I bought your mother a ring for our tenth anniversary. She wanted a big diamond. We found something we loved and could afford, and I took it to be appraised while she waited at the jeweler's as collateral."

Really? I wonder. This is a story I never heard before.

Did it happen as Dad remembers it, Mom sitting by passively while Dad takes charge? These are behaviors that don't fit my ideas of either of them. But does it matter? What matters is that on this day of romance and connection, Dad is remembering his bride and sweet times they shared.

Our memories, it has been said, can bring roses in winter and allow us to revisit love in the coldest and darkest of times—even on Valentine's Day.

BABY STEPS
March 15, 2004

A few times a week Summerwood organizes an outing, some special event that takes residents out into the world for a cultural or culinary treat.

At breakfast, Sam turns to Isabel, a shy, self-effacing Polish woman, and asks, "Why didn't you join us at the state capital yesterday? They put on a terrific show, honoring immigrants."

Isabel lost her husband to brain cancer six months ago, before she moved into Summerwood, and she hasn't begun to socialize. She glances down at her wedding band and says sheepishly, "Because I didn't want to go alone."

"You're not alone," Murray chimes in. "You go on the Summerwood bus. Everyone's together."

Dad inserts his friendly two cents: "You have to sign up

on the second floor. There's a concert at seven-thirty tomor-row at the University of Hartford."

Dad amazes me. When did he become such an expert in independent living? I always thought Sam organized his time. Or me. And before that, Mom. But circumstances have changed. He's on his own now.

It's like camp, this Summerwood, only it's not just for the summer, it's for life, what remains of it. At Camp Sum-merwood, Dad, once the master of helplessness, mentors the novice. Isabel, the grieving widow, once isolated and de-pressed, has come down for breakfast for the first time, and tasted a sense of belonging, an expanded sense of self. Mov-ing in and moving on, fitting in and finding your way—these are the challenges for everyone in a home for the aged.

Isabel turns to Dad and exclaims, "I would love to go to a concert. I'm so embarrassed I didn't know about the sign-ups."

"That's why you come to breakfast—to talk over what's happening," Dad says.

When the last bowl of hot cereal is polished off, we all make our way to the elevator.

"Now be sure to get off at the second floor to sign up for the concert," I remind Isabel.

"I will," she answers. "Later."

She presses "3" and heads back to her room.

A Nice Fruit Salad
April 28, 2004

The topic of conversation at Summerwood this morning is the cost of fruit salad.

A breakfast buffet is included in the monthly fee, and many residents, watching their budgets, have taken to smuggling a dish of fruit salad to their rooms to eat later in the day, perhaps as a substitute for lunch, which is not included in the meal plan. In retaliation, Summerwood has announced a policy change: from now on, residents who take a bowl of fruit from the breakfast room will have to pay for it.

"If they're going to charge me for taking food to my room, then I want them to deduct the cost of the food I don't eat in the dining room," Sam bristles. "I often miss dinners. Why should I have to pay extra for fruit salad?"

Residents are allowed to miss up to four dinners a month, free of charge. After that, they're billed, whether they show up or not.

Dad and I gnaw on our bagels, caught in the cross fire, amused by the sparks that fly across the table. This group could use a little entertainment, a heated debate to warm up the day.

Isabel, now a breakfast regular, whispers to Dad, "How much do they charge for fruit salad?"

"Seventy-five cents. A banana alone is twenty-five cents."
"It's worth it, don't you think?"

The two of them grin generously at each other.

"If I have to pay for this, I might as well get my money's worth," Isabel says playfully, as she heads to the buffet.

"Fill it up to the top!" Sam urges her.

Isabel giggles and piles her bowl with fruit. Clutching her bounty, she strides out the door.

Sam belts out, "You stay out of trouble!"

"I'll try," Isabel replies dryly. "But it's not easy."

ENGAGEMENT PARTY
May 7, 2004

It's a bright, breezy May day, and Marc, my first husband, is throwing an engagement party for our son Aaron and his fiancée, Ali, at his tony West Hartford home. The jubilant couple mingles among relatives and friends, and basks in their affection. For me, though, it's a time of high drama as I struggle to interact with the people who deserted me more than two decades ago.

Dad shuffles into the living room where everyone is gathering and lowers himself into an overstuffed chair. There he remains for most of the day, radiating positive energy, genially greeting everyone who approaches him. He looks spiffy in his new beige linen Brooks Brothers jacket, sky-blue polo shirt, and navy gabardine pants. With luck and good medicine, he'll be wearing this outfit to Aaron's wedding fourteen months from now.

Ali comes over and offers Dad her ring finger to inspect. "It looks very nice on you," he says approvingly.

Ali's mother, Debbie, Aaron's future *machatonister* (mother-in-law), sidles up to Dad. This is their first meeting. "May I kiss you?" she asks, bending down and planting her lips on his cheek.

"You're a very good kisser," he says, glowing.

And so the day unfolds. One by one, specters from a former life step forward to say hello and wish me and Dad well, and one by one, I make the requisite gestures, kissing them, inquiring about their lives. Inside, though, I'm rattled. The woman Marc left me for—and then divorced—comes over to Dad and wraps her arms around him. Dad hugs her back. Marc's mother and sister come by, too. Complicated relationships—shredded by divorce, an ugly custody battle, and financial disputes—are pieced back together by the power of a ring.

I'm thrown when I see Ivy, the housekeeper who raised my kids, now eighty-two. When Marc set up his new home with Wife Number Two, Ivy moved in with him. Forgiveness still eludes me. Dad's eyes tear when he sees her. What is he crying for? A time past? A time we all survived? A soft spot in his heart for the woman who helped steer his grandchildren through a domestic storm?

We're all here, interacting like a family, and Dad is here, too, nibbling on crudités, taking it all in. Does he forgive these people who hurt his family so deeply? He appears unruffled and exudes an air of warm acceptance, creating a zone around him where everyone feels comfortable and safe.

Research shows that as people age they tend to forgive more easily. How do they do it? Is it that, nearing the end of their lives, they opt to pack lighter, refusing to take their bitterness or sorrow with them to the grave? Have they swallowed enough disappointment over the years to learn not to choke on it? Has time dulled the pain or taught them to expect less from others? Perhaps they've learned to rewrite the traumatic narrative, incorporating other points of view. However they accomplish it, they decide to move beyond their grievances and try to enjoy what's left of the journey.

This makes sense to me. Surely it would be a crime to live such a joyous moment in a grudge state. Taking Dad's lead, I steady myself, make the best of the day in honor of my son, and pass around the tray of shrimp.

Muriel
May 14, 2004

Muriel has as much pep and passion as anyone could pack into a four-and-a-half-foot, ninety-pound frame. She races around like a girl on roller skates, always animated, always ready for conversation. The outfits she wears reflect her teenage years—cotton blouses made of tiny floral prints, matching solid color cardigans, and A-line skirts. Today, however, her skirts have an elastic waist to accommodate her swelling abdomen, and her sneakers look more orthopedic than athletic.

At breakfast, she comes up to me and shares the bad news. "I lost my best friend today. She was ninety-five. She was feeling tired. The doctor misdiagnosed her. Her heart stopped. I guess doctors sometimes make mistakes."

Muriel pauses to take it all in, then continues. "This week I celebrated my ninety-fourth birthday. My other friends took me out to lunch. I've got wonderful friends, but . . . this was my *closest* friend."

She peers into my eyes, as though to gain strength through connection. I wonder what on earth I can say to console her.

"It must be very hard," I acknowledge lamely, bending down to hug her. She holds on tightly, then says, "Thank you," and walks away.

I look around. Everyone here has been touched by death. Residents return at night to empty apartments. Dad's neighbor, Rose Goldfarb, was taken to the hospital last week and won't be back. Manny Schwartz, the man Dad trumped at bridge on Thursday, was carried unconscious from his room yesterday at dawn. A note is tacked to the board by the front desk: the van is leaving for Manny's funeral at eleven. Another note says that one more man is needed to say kaddish for Sally Bushman.

Spouses gone. Friends and family gone. The message is clear: death makes no exceptions. Death is for you, and me, too.

A Trip to Goodspeed
May 16, 2004

Summer stock is good for the soul, so Michael and I take Dad on a family outing to the Goodspeed Opera House, a Victorian confection rising majestically above the banks of the Connecticut River. Today's performance? *Call Me Madam.*

Sister Sue and her husband, Mort, are waiting for us at an Italian café across from the theater. It's good being with family—conversation ripples along as inexorably as the river.

We sit outdoors soaking up the extra-virgin olive oil and the sun. The waiter brings Dad a plate piled high with spaghetti marinara and shrimp. He gets more on his khaki pants than in his mouth, but his pleasure is mine. I try to save his cardigan sweater with a wad of napkins, and give up.

Sue rolls her eyes, sympathetically. Her parents were old once, too.

"So, Lou, would you like someone to stay with you full-time?" Mort asks politely.

"It depends what she looks like," he quips.

Dad is tickled by his joke. We all break out laughing. A young girl at the next table catches our silliness and beams back a smileful of lasagna.

This is an Ecclesiastes moment—a time to laugh, a time to sing.

Shavuot
May 24, 2004

At breakfast I announce that Dad and I are heading over to the Jewish Center for a swim—or more exactly, a walk in the water.

"Don't bother," says Izzy. "It's Shavuot. The center will be closed."

"What's Shavuot?" I ask, trying to recall its significance, happy to take a lesson from the pro.

"There are three important Jewish holidays," Izzy says, clearing his throat. "Pesach, Rosh Hashanah, and Shavuot."

"But what's it about?" I ask.

Izzy looks at me blankly.

"I think it's about spring," another tablemate chimes in.

I stop Dad's friend Rose, well up into her nineties, on her way to the blintzes. "Rose, help us out. What's the meaning of Shavuot?"

She shrugs. "I give up. What's the answer?"

Dad chuckles. "People go to shul on this day for eighty, ninety years and no one knows why."

I can see the irony in it, too. We all go through life following the rituals and rules, seldom stopping to ask, "What's it about?"

I wipe the jam off Dad's face and bring him to the computer room to consult my spiritual adviser—Google.com. Shavuot, I learn, is indeed a celebration of the season. It also commemorates the passing down of the Ten Commandments, and is a time to rededicate ourselves to the teaching of the Torah.

On our way back to Dad's apartment, we run into Rose again, pushing her walker with arthritic slowness.

"How're you doing?" Dad asks her.

"Excellent. Every day a little bit better." She smiles impishly and pauses to catch her breath. "I'm off to visit my parents. My daughter is picking me up to take me to the cemetery."

"Shavuot celebrates the Ten Commandments," I say, proud of my newfound wisdom. "Number Five: Honor your father and mother."

"I didn't know that," Rose admits.

"God will forgive you," I say.

"Happy Shavuot," Dad joins in.

"Happy Shavuot to you, too," Rose replies.

I want to share with her another bit of truth I've picked up today: you don't need to know the meaning of a holiday to live it. But she's already on her way out the door.

PRIVATE PARTS
May 24, 2004

I bring Dad to an indoor town pool that's open on Shavuot. The boy at the desk has a guileless face and the sinuous arms of a swimmer. "Do you live in West Hartford?" he asks, looking up from a dog-eared copy of *Walden*.

"My father does."

"Bring him back after one, okay? We're open to the community then, okay?"

I look into the pool area. It's huge. A solitary figure cuts through the water, leaving a diaphanous wake. The air is drenched in chlorine and sweat.

"My dad is eighty-four. He naps in the afternoon. Could I take him in for a half hour now? He usually swims at the Jewish Community Center, but it's closed today."

The boy studies us. "I guess so." He motions down the hall. "There's a family room on the left. You can go in there with him, okay?"

Now here's someone else who understands the spirit of Shavuot.

Dad lets me help him out of his clothes. When he's down to his underwear he points to the door, and I retreat to the ladies' room across the hall, slip into my suit, and wait. Images of him sprawled unconscious on the floor cross my obsessive mind. Finally, the door opens. There he stands, in his baggy swim suit, bent forward, balancing on his spindly legs, an air of triumph on his face. "Look at me," his smile says, "I changed into my suit myself."

Dad's chest ripples, a field of soft white fur. His breasts sag. Time has played its tricks on him, but he's still a handsome man. I take his arm and help him across the slick, slippery tiles and into the water. It's bathtub warm—perfect for his arthritis, his Parkinson's, his spirits, and mine.

"How's it working out with your new neighbor?" I ask. "The one whose dog barks when she leaves her apartment."

"It's the cutest little thing, but, boy, can it yap."

"What's happening this week?"

"Sam signed me up for a jazz concert at Hall High. You should hear those kids play. Like professionals."

"Winning any bridge games these days?"

"Yeah, but my partner, Eve, keeps falling asleep at the table and dropping her cards."

Back and forth we go, pushing our way through the waist-high water, the words flowing easily between us.

In the changing room, Dad points me again to the door. "That's okay," I say. "I won't look. You got something special going on there you don't want me to see?"

"Ha," he chortles. I get down on my knees behind him, pull down his trunks, and wipe his wet rear end with a towel. I don't look. Who wants to? As far as I'm concerned, private parts are private, even if everything else about this man's life is an open book, and I'm reading it page by page.

THE GIFT
May 26, 2004

"Would you like to hear me speak on May twenty-sixth?" I asked Dad a month ago. "The Brandeis Women's Committee has invited me to top off their luncheon with a talk on forgiveness."

"Call me on May twenty-fifth," he quipped.

When I swing by Dad's apartment, he's dressed to go. We're greeted at the restaurant by a gaggle of fifty or so Jewish women, encased in their finest bouclé suits. I wheel Dad to the head table and seat him facing the podium, surrounded by several of my close friends. While I sign books, the ladies fuss over him. He says something I can't hear, and they burst out laughing.

Knowing Dad would be joining me, I spent an insane amount of time polishing and rehearsing my speech. Finally, the time has come. The glazed salmon and butter balls are cleared away. I'm introduced, and I introduce Dad, not that he's a stranger to anyone.

My talk goes well. I return to the table and give Dad a kiss. He leans over and whispers in my ear, "I used to think your education was expensive. Now I see, it was a bargain."

I'm touched. Is there a more precious gift a parent can give a child than words of praise?

As we head back to Summerwood, I think of all the sacrifices my parents made to set me up for life, all the handouts I accepted, as though they were my right. What would it cost me to acknowledge my debt?

Is there a more precious gift a child can give a parent than words of gratitude?

I turn to Dad to thank him, but his eyes are closed and his head is bobbing on his chest. We'll talk later, I'm sure.

FIVE MORE YEARS

June 4, 2004

"Bye, Pop," I say, hugging Dad in his big green recliner. Replays of the Ryder Cup Tournament roll across the television screen as I head to the door. Dad smiles and waves weakly.

Out in the hallway I can't stop the tears. With each visit he looks more and more slumped over, as though his head is filled with stones. His spine curves forward like a big question mark, and his muscles are both soft from lack of exercise and stiff from Parkinson's, which is winning the game. I'm exhausted, lifting him in and out of his wheelchair, schlepping him to doctors, filling the silences with conversation. I hear the clock ticking.

If Dad dies in the next five years, I don't know how I'll
stand it. If he lives for another five years, I don't know how
I'll stand it.

Robin

*"My father's colon cancer has returned," a patient named
Robin tells me. Her healthy glow belies her emotional
fragility. "The chemo didn't work, and the doctors aren't
optimistic. He's only seventy-seven. I can't imagine life
without him."*

*Robin's eyes well up, and she begins to sob. "He's been
the best dad in the world. My rock. How will I go on when
he's gone? How do people do it—losing someone they love
so much?"*

*I sit facing Robin, paralyzed. Should I tell her the
truth—that I ask myself the same question every day and
have no answer? I could tell her I know what it's like
to feel terrified and alone, but why burden her with my
story?*

*"Robin," I begin, "losing a father you love so much is
an incalculable loss. But if you paint him as a saint you'll
exaggerate that loss and make it harder for you to separate from him. I'm not saying your love isn't real, but living apart, seeing him only from time to time, you may
have made him larger than life and turned him from the
father he was into the father you wanted him to be. To
carry on without him, to let him go, you need to dethrone*

*him, and separate the man from the myth. I encour-
age you to ask yourself: 'By magnifying his role in my
life, am I underestimating my ability to function without
him?' It would be good to remind yourself that you're no
longer a small, helpless child, alone in the world. You
have a network of close friends to support you, and a
thriving career. I don't mean to minimize your father's
importance in your life, but I don't want you to minimize your resourcefulness, either. You've done so much on
your own."*

*Robin brushes the hair back from her eyes. "Ratio-
nally, I know what you're saying is true," she concedes. "I
even know that Dad isn't perfect and hasn't always been
there for me. But emotionally I feel like I'm falling from
the sky with no net to catch me."*

*"Robin, there's a saying that may help you during this
terrible time: 'People die, relationships don't.' Does that
mean anything to you?"*

*"You're saying my father will die but my relationship
with him will last forever?"*

*"Yes, when a person dies you lose their body but not
their imprint on your life. When your father leaves this
world, everything about him—his humor, his belief in
you, his delight in your specialness—will continue to live
on inside you, and through you. I promise."*

*The session is over. Robin stands to leave. "You've
been helpful," she says.*

*It goes both ways, I'm thinking. As I find the words to
help you, I help myself.*

THE EMERGENCY ROOM
June 21, 2004

The call comes early. "This is Summerwood. Your dad isn't well. It could be a cold. He's in bed and can't sit up."

My first patient rings the bell. "I'm sorry," I explain. "I have an emergency. My father . . ."

"Go ahead, do what you have to," she counsels me. I know she understands. Her mother is failing, too. We belong to the same sorority of caregivers.

I race to West Hartford and find Dad lying limply in bed. Sitting beside him, babysitting, is his buddy Dave. "I'm just making sure he's okay," Dave says, modestly. "He fell last night and hit his head."

"No patients today?" Dad asks me.

"You're my patient today," I answer smoothly, dismissing thoughts of anxious clients and lost income.

Dad is admitted to Hartford Hospital without formalities, wrapped in a thin cotton gown and laid out on a gurney in a private room. I'm searching for a blanket when he announces he has to pee.

I press the button above his head.

The intercom crackles. "Yes?"

"My dad has to go to the bathroom."

"A nurse will be there shortly."

Ten minutes pass. Another ten. I ring again. A voice reassures me that an aide is on her way.

Dad looks at me anxiously.

"Okay, we'll figure this out."

I open the closet door and find a plastic bottle. *Let's give the man some dignity. He's about to pee all over himself.*

I open his fly, reach in, pull out his soft, lanky penis, and stuff its head into the pee bottle. Relieved, he goes.

This modest man, who just one month ago refused to let me near him when he undressed, now doesn't seem to notice or mind. Privacy is a luxury he can no longer afford. What a change, what a falling off.

When Dad and I went swimming on Shavuot, I averted my eyes from his penis, but here, in the hospital, I can't help peeking at it. It's quite large, actually, with a plump head, and nicely shaped. I expected it to look more shriveled up. It's from this I was born. How extraordinary is the miracle of life. And how ordinary.

I flash back to my childhood. I'm eight. Mom and Dad have gone to bed suspiciously early. My brother and I are supposed to be down in the den watching *Jeopardy!* but I've snuck upstairs and crawled under the sewing machine outside their door to listen. Dad is doing something awful to Mom, but she isn't complaining. He's speaking dirty to her, and she's moaning and swearing. I'm fascinated and frozen with fear. Suddenly, Mom blurts out, "Janis is listening," and I dash into my bedroom and pull the covers up over my head.

Today as I hold my father's penis, this forbidden object, in my hand, there are no more secrets, no more mysteries. I take the bottle from Dad and flush his urine down the drain. It disappears with a roar. Suddenly, I feel weird, creepy, as though I've broken a commandment, and await the wrath of God. It's strange to have such intimate contact with your father. It's also sad.

This is it, isn't it? The final regression. When a parent reaches this level of dependence, we're nearing the end of the line.

The Lesson
July 20, 2004

When I was a kid, Dad took me ice skating in Elizabeth Park. The frozen pond was open to the public, deep into the night, way past my bedtime. First stop was a grungy snack bar serving pizza so hot and spicy, you'd think the stars were dancing in your mouth. Then Dad sat me down on a park bench, and, kneeling over me, patiently tied up my long, white laces. All bundled up, we waddled together into the bright lights. Dad skated backward at first, pulling me toward him, showing me how to turn and stop. When he finally let go, I felt free and excited and a little scared as I slipped across the cold crystal floor.

Turn the clock ahead fifty years, reverse the seasons, and

here we are on a balmy summer day, back in Elizabeth Park. I carefully help Dad out of the car, patiently repeating directions I've given him countless times: how to grab the door and pull himself up, how to rotate his rear end and lower himself into the wheelchair. I kneel down to adjust the Velcro tabs on his sneakers, then wheel him over to our favorite spot, a patch of soft grassy shade among beds of specimen roses.

Life has come full circle, it seems. The child has become the parent; the parent, the child. But the analogy is misleading. As a parent, you invest in your children's future. If they're healthy, you can expect them to grow and thrive. Your freedom comes with their independence. It's a life-affirming transformation for both of you.

Caring for an elderly father or mother is another story. You invest time and patience only to see them regress and become more helpless and disabled. Your release is paid for with their lives. There is no next chapter.

THE WALKER
August 10, 2004

I'm filling the kiddush cup when the bell rings. It's Sister Sue with Dad in tow for Passover dinner. Dad doesn't know it, but a walker is waiting for him in the living room.

Getting around has become treacherous business for Dad. His Parkinson's makes his movements rigid and jerky. A sticky substance occupies the neural synapses of his brain, like glue on the bottom of a shoe. His feet seem to hug the floor; lifting them takes a conscious effort. Last spring, when I suggested we check out a walker, he wouldn't hear of it. "No walker!" he insisted, meaning, "Don't treat me like an old man. I'm still alive and kicking."

The model I picked out for him is a snazzy metallic blue, with three wheels, hand brakes, and a pouch just right for necessities—a box of tissues, a water bottle, sunglasses, baseball cap, and wallet. The heavier models come with a seat you can use when you feel weak or dizzy or just need to get off your feet—the perfect answer for the quarter-mile trek around the Summerwood property—but I've opted for the lighter version that Dad can fold and lift into a car or van.

My younger son Max grabs hold of the walker and takes it for a spin around the room, trying to lighten the mood.

Dad eyes it suspiciously.

"Try it, Louie," Max says, parking it in front of him.

Dad looks at everyone looking at him and wraps his fleshy fingers around the handlebars. Slowly he shuffles along, testing his new mobility. The family goads him on and follows him down the hallway: "Push that mother." "Now you're rollin'." "There he goes, the Pied Piper of Pesach!"

"I don't need this," he insists. "Take it back." But he tightens his grip and pushes forward.

"You don't have to keep it," I say, disingenuously, "but why not try it for a few weeks? Pretend it's a shopping cart. It's good for your posture."

As Dad continues haltingly, he breaks into a smile, like a baby who has just taken his first steps, or a teen who is trying out his new wheels.

That was four months ago. Today the walker, which Dad rejected so vehemently, is indispensable. There is no option, no debate. Dad needs it to reach down for an Eskimo Pie in his freezer, to join the men for dinner, to hoist himself up from his chair and prepare for bed. With three new, sturdy legs he's less likely to trip and wind up in the hospital . . . or the morgue.

Given Dad's deterioration, it's neither noble nor courageous for him to rail against old age; it's dangerous and dumb. I'm thrilled that he's given up the protest.

Why then do I feel so down?

EARLY ALZHEIMER'S
September 5–6, 2004

I'm still on the plane when I call Dad to let him know I've made it home from Argentina.

"How was Buenos Aires?" he asks, sounding clear and focused.

"Wow," I answer. "You're too much, Pop. How did you remember Buenos Aires? We had a great time."

"Did you take any tango lessons?"

"We did. And boy, is it tough to learn those fancy steps!"

"So, when are you coming to visit? Today's Wednesday. Are you coming tomorrow?"

"I am, but today is Thursday. Tomorrow is Friday."

"That's fine," he answers.

I hang up and call Michael. "Dad's in great spirits," I report, "and his mind is razor sharp, except he thought today was Wednesday. I suppose when you're living at Summerwood, it doesn't matter what day of the week it is."

"But your father's right," Michael observes. "Today *is* Wednesday."

The next morning—Thursday—Sam asks me, over a bowl of oatmeal, "How's Bill?"

"Bill?" I repeat. "You mean my husband, Marc . . . ?"

"Marc?" Sam rummages through his memory and comes up empty-handed.

I correct myself. "I mean Michael. Marc and I have been divorced for nineteen years."

"Sounds like you're ready for Summerwood," Sam jokes.

He's not far off. I should put my name on the waiting list. When the residents struggle to remember a word or recent event, I feel superior. When they wax wistfully about my vitality and good looks, I lap it up. But there are moments like now when I feel my age stalking me. I get a glimpse of the future, and it's not pretty.

More Secrets
September 25, 2004

Dad pees incessantly, sometimes every twenty minutes, day and night. He has also developed unbearable pain in his lower back, which has made him even more sedentary than usual. Pain medications help, but they all come with nasty side effects—dizziness, nausea, a proneness to falling. His world has shrunk to the confines of his chair or bed.

The results come back from radiology: Dad's cancer has metastasized to his bones. Dr. Kosto, his urologist, is going to give him a Lupron injection every three or four months to see if it helps. Lupron is a hormone that can slow or stop the growth of cancerous cells and relieve some of the symptoms.

"What do you think?" I ask the doctor. "Do I tell him his cancer has spread?"

Dr. Kosto has been my father's urologist since the 1980s, when he treated Dad for prostate and bladder cancers. The doctor must be pushing eighty himself. I trust him. His judgment is sound, and he knows Dad well.

"I wouldn't. It would just upset him."

"What about the peeing?"

Dr. Kosto hands me a night catheter. "Do you know how to use this?"

"I could guess."

"You slip the condom on his penis and his urine goes down into the bag."

I agree to take the contraption home, knowing there's no way in hell Dad is going to let someone put it on him, and no way he can manage it himself. I make a mental note to call the pharmacy and have them send Dad a few boxes of Depends.

"You know," I tell Dr. Kosto, "we're not looking for miracles here. But my son Aaron is getting married in nine months and it would mean the world to all of us to have Dad there."

I gag back the tears. Dr. Kosto tries to reassure me. "We'll do our best."

Dad looks up from the ninth hole at Pebble Beach. "So that test I took," he asks me, "the results were good?"

I look at him blankly, my mind whirling. A moment of truth. What do I tell him: your cancer has infiltrated your bones? Will it help him to know? Does he really want to know? Dad has taken innumerable tests and never asked about them before. Do I have the right to keep bad news from him? Wouldn't the truth give him time to say good-bye to the people he loves and ready himself for whatever lies ahead? If it were me, I would insist my kids tell me everything.

"You're having a problem, but not a big problem," I say, fudging the truth. "Dr. Kosto is going to give you an injection that should make you feel better. So, how about some lunch? There's a new pizza parlor up the street. You hungry?"

"Not really," he answers.

I don't ask him what he's thinking because I don't want him asking me what I'm thinking.

CAR TALK
October 30, 2004

On a cold October day, Dad's car battery dies in the Summerwood parking lot. Instead of heading home, I hang out in his apartment, waiting for AAA: another hundred bucks down the drain.

Passing time, Dad tells me about his first adventure behind the wheel. He was fifteen when his mother declared, "I'm taking a trip to Niagara Falls. Want to come?"

Dad's mother, Rose, was a zesty character, fearless and game. She must have been, taking off like that on a whim in 1934, leaving her husband at home to fend for himself.

"In those days, it was a much longer drive from Bridgeport to Niagara Falls," Dad reminisces, his eyes full of mischief. "When we crossed into New York, I asked my mother, 'Can I take over?' and she said, 'Go ahead.' It wasn't long before I saw flashing lights. Oh boy, what a mess. We got pulled over and fined, and that ended my driving career for a while."

Dad laughs, reliving his boyhood experience. How great to be a little reckless, a little foolish—to get behind the wheel and zoom off. No wonder he refuses to turn in his car—he'd have to admit he's over the hill, no longer safe on the road, to himself or others. He would become a prisoner to the kindness of those at Summerwood who drive, and forfeit any chance of following a bold, youthful impulse to shift into gear and escape from an old-age home.

"I remember when I took my mother's keys away," Dad says. "I told her, 'What if you stop using the car for a week—give it up a little at a time?' "

"That's a great idea," I exclaim.

"My mother fought like hell. She was miserable."

"I'm sure it was hard for both of you."

"I'm not ready to give up my car."

"Last month you fell asleep at the wheel and woke up in the soft shoulder. You could have killed yourself, or someone else."

"I know it."

"You could have been sued for millions."

"I know it."

"Someone saw you driving out of the parking lot Sunday with the door wide open."

"It only happened once."

"With what you spend on insurance, gas, and maintenance, you could take a cab anywhere you want, and save a fortune."

Dad looks miserable. He has had enough of my meddling.

I plead with him. "If I leave the number of the local cab company on your table, will you try it a few times?"

"I need my car."

"Dad, Joel's car just died. You could give him yours. He'd love it. . . ."

No response.

"Winter is coming. You're not going to drive on snow and ice. It's a pain having someone clean your car each time it snows, and move it so Summerwood can plow your parking space. The air-conditioning is useless, and so is the radio."

I take out the title to his car and hand it to him. I've had it in my pocketbook for weeks. "I'd like you to sign this," I say.

He complies without a murmur.

"Are you okay giving the car to Joel and Janice?" I ask, pretending to be democratic.

"I'm okay."

He hands me the keys, and that's it. We both know he'll never drive again.

Such is the natural order of things: his mother handed him the keys. He took them away from her. Dad handed me the keys. Now I take them away from him. This is the way it happens. What has been done will be done again. There is nothing new at Summerwood, or anywhere else under the sun.

DIAL-A-RIDE
December 1 and 4, 2004

On Monday, I call Dad's apartment and find him home alone, watching TV.

"What are you doing there, Dad?" I ask. "How come you didn't go to bridge?"

"I forgot to call in time," he tells me. "I called on Friday instead of Thursday."

Dad is referring to Dial-a-Ride, a community service that transports senior citizens for a small fee. Since Dad gave up driving, he has begun to take their van to the senior center in West Hartford on Monday and Thursday afternoons to play bridge. Dial-a-Ride's rule is you need to call two business days in advance to arrange for transportation.

"Did Annie go?" I ask.

"Yeah. She told me the van was half-empty."

Annie is another resident at Summerwood who takes the van to the center to play cards. She's older than Dad, I'd say around ninety. But she seems more on top of things, sharper. Later I look up her number in the resident phone book and call to ask if she'd mind reserving a space for Dad on the van when she calls for herself. "I'd be happy to," she tells me. "Your father is very good company."

On Thursday, I call Dad. He's alone again in front of the TV.

"What happened now?" I ask.

"Dial-a-Ride won't let someone else call for me. I have to call myself. I can do that, but sometimes I forget."

I call Dial-a-Ride, wild with anger. I'm ready to strangle the operator but appeal instead to her intelligence and humanity.

"I understand your policy and know you have limited resources and need to plan ahead," I start, "but my father has had strokes and sometimes can't remember to call on a certain day. Annie Birnbaum calls to be picked up every Monday and Thursday at noon. Can you make an exception and let her call for both of them?"

"No," the operator says. "Your dad has to call himself, two days in advance."

I begin to unravel. "Do you understand that my dad is, in effect, brain damaged and *can't* follow your rules? I thought you were offering a community service to the elderly, giving them a little independence, a few hours of fun."

"That's true," the operator says flatly, "but he has to call himself, two days in advance."

"What is it exactly you don't understand about someone who is brain damaged?" I hiss. "Are *you* brain damaged?" I slam down the phone, angry at myself for losing control, angry at the stupidity of a policy that's so grossly insensitive to the people it's meant to serve, angry at the damn lady who's probably as helpless as I am.

Okay, okay, I tell myself, trying to calm down. I'll remind Dad whenever he needs to book a ride. No problem. I'm not sure I'll remember either, but sometimes you just have to play the hand you're dealt, whether you like the cards or not.

THE BIRTHDAY PARTY
December 18, 2004

On most days, the public areas at Summerwood are empty, but when there's a social event, residents pour out of the woodwork looking for a good time. It strikes me, why not have a birthday party for Dad and invite everyone?

Summerwood agrees to circulate a notice to its seventy-four residents: "Come celebrate Louis Lieff's 85th birthday in the café at 2 p.m. on Sunday. Refreshments will be provided by the family, followed by a video of Frank Sinatra, Judy Garland, and Dean Martin singing and dancing."

Early in the morning, Michael and I pick up a kosher chocolate layer cake at the Crown, with the words "POP 85!" inscribed in shimmering turquoise frosting. We set it down on the buffet, along with sodas, paper plates, and plastic forks. By the time I wheel Dad off the elevator, dozens of people are waiting to greet us. The place is buzzing with excitement.

I'm touched that so many residents have joined in the celebration. So is Dad.

"You're kidding," he says, looking around.

Michael and I take requests from those who can't make it to the buffet themselves or don't have an aide to help them.

"Is the cake kosher?" one woman asks.

"Do you have diet ginger ale?" asks another, as I pick up my pace.

"I want Coke."

"Do you have ice?"

"Hey, miss, when will I get a piece?"

Some of the guests are lost in themselves, grabbing whatever they can get, but most are courteous and grateful, wanting nothing more than to join in the festivities and escape the tedium of their lives. In the company of others, they seem to become whole and rooted again.

Someone taps my elbow. It's Sid, a frail, nearly blind, eighty-nine-year-old friend of Dad—his golf partner in the Day's When. "I want to say a few words," he announces.

Sid's voice is as fragile as glass. So is his body. When I run into him, he often rambles on about the past. I panic. *Oh, God. He doesn't look well enough to pull it off. He's going to ruin the party.*

"That's nice of you, Sid," I blurt out, "but there's no need to say anything."

Sid insists, or perhaps he doesn't hear me, and pushes his walker slowly across the length of the room to where Dad is seated. A snail pushing a stone.

"That's okay, Sid. You can speak from where you are."

Sid finally reaches Dad and places a quivering hand on his shoulder. "Lou has been a good friend for fifty years," Sid begins, in a voice that wobbles but is clear and warm. "He's so good-natured and kind, so honest and decent. And a hell of a good dancer! I'll never forget when he hit a hole in one at Cliffside Country Club. We were so excited, we left our clubs on the course." Sid shares a few more memories, then inches his way back to his seat. Dad's eyes shine with laughter and tears.

After singing "Happy Birthday" and polishing off the last piece of cake, the residents make their way to the recreation room with its huge TV. Dad follows, pushing his walker with a big smile, rotating his body slowly, like a dancer.

We arrange ourselves around the screen, where Judy, Frank, and Dean belt out their songs in a legendary 1962 TV special in grainy black and white. The three are smooth and naughty, all at the top of their game.

The video is long, maybe ninety minutes, but no one leaves early. Some fall asleep in their chairs or wheelchairs, but most of them snap their fingers to the tunes and croon along, spirits soaring. These are songs from their era, a time when most of them had steady legs and strong partnerships.

I look around the room and can't help seeing so much loss—loss of loved ones, loss of health, loss of dreams. But I also see so much life—all these people trying to make the best of a Sunday afternoon, consigned to a new, ready-made family of friends in this home-away-from-home called Summerwood.

I scroll ahead and see myself sitting alone in a continuing-care facility, thinking back on my life with Michael. Will I rise to the challenge? Will I remember the good times we shared, without falling into despair over what remains?

My response to Sid, I realize—my effort to shush him up

and shunt him into a corner—was a deplorable display of prejudice against the elderly. "Ageism" is what Robert Butler calls it in *Why Survive?*—a process by which we, the younger generations, systematically stereotype and discriminate against the old, refusing to identify with them as fellow human beings.

Shame on me, and hurrah for Sid and all the residents of Summerwood who have come out for Dad's birthday. They remind me that friendship and joy can endure the blows of age. I applaud them for kicking up their heels even if they can hardly lift their feet.

FORGIVENESS
December 20, 2004

Throughout my first marriage, my mother-in-law, Phyllis, and I respected and loved each other in ways we both failed miserably at conveying. When her son Marc pulled the plug on our marriage, our families ostensibly stopped talking to each other. There were occasions—birthdays, bar mitzvahs, my son's engagement party—when everyone tried to be cordial, but deep hurts lay beneath the surface that were never addressed and never resolved.

Two weeks ago, Phyllis called Dad to wish him mazel tov on his eighty-fifth birthday. They hadn't spoken to each other in any meaningful way in more than twenty years.

This morning, at my suggestion, Dad called Phyllis to wish her the best on *her* eighty-fifth. He phoned to let me know.

"I'm sure she was delighted to hear from you," I say.

"It was good I called," he acknowledges.

Taking my own advice, I pick up the phone and call Phyllis myself. "I don't understand what happened between us," I say. "You meant so much to me. I never understood why you didn't call . . ."

In the past, we kept our conversations light and superficial. Today, however, after a brief exchange of birthday greetings and news about the kids, we begin to talk through our misunderstandings and missteps, and gently redress the grievances of the past.

It would be easier to keep our distance and cling to our "official" stories, our personal versions of the truth, the ones that have protected us all these years from knowing our frailties, our flaws. But now, as we stand before death, we both know the door is closing. So while there's still some possibility of renewal, we step forward and join Dad in the healing circle. A few heartfelt words forge a path to forgiveness.

This is a time to reach out, to accept each other's limitations, to appreciate each other's goodness, to grow healthy tissue over old sores. This is a time to let go, to let in, to reconnect, while there's still life to breathe.

If not now, when?

Forgiveness Redux

I'm interviewed on the radio—the topic, forgiveness. A woman calls in, asking for advice: "My father is dying in hospice," she tells me. "I don't believe he loves me, and I must confess, I haven't always been that lovable. Can we make peace this late in the day? Where do I begin?"

"I'd start off apologizing for the specific ways you've *hurt* him.*"*

"And accepting all the blame?"

"If you go first, you cut a path to forgiveness, and your dad may follow. Even if he turns away, you'll respect yourself for owning up to your complicity. You know what you've done wrong, and you'll live with your guilt until you try to make things right. Once you apologize, you can let your father know exactly how he has injured you. I call this 'locating your pain.' Try to speak in a soft, respectful tone, because if you club him with your resentment, he's going to retaliate or recoil. The way you send a message is the way it comes back.

"You might say, 'There's something I'd like to address that hurts me very much. I'm not bringing it up to upset you but to soften things between us. Would you like to hear me out?' If he says okay, you could tell him, 'I don't know if you love me, or if you ever have. I'm not asking you to make something up, but if there is love in your heart for me, it would mean the world to hear it from you.'

"Don't assume that your father doesn't want to repair

the damage between you, or that he knows what you need to heal. Don't assume he even knows he has hurt you. By confronting the truth, you may confirm your worst fear, that he doesn't love you, but you also give him a chance to make good. Wouldn't it be wonderful if the two of you could cleanse and bind your wounds before he dies?"

I hang up and wonder what will happen to this woman. Will she reach out to her father and create an opportunity for them to earn each other's forgiveness?

If not now, when?

WHO ARE YOU?
January 12, 2005

The emergency room is throbbing with activity as sick people cry out in pain or stare blankly into space. Gurneys are lined up in the hallway like cars waiting for gas. Dad is one of the lucky ones, assigned a room he only has to share with one neatly bandaged man. Last night, on his way to the bathroom, Dad fell hard, and the first set of X-rays revealed a broken shoulder. The doctor put him on morphine to control the pain and inserted a catheter in his penis. I pull the curtain around him to give him some privacy, then draw up a chair and wait for the next step.

"Those draperies," Dad says to me with an agitated, delirious look. "I made them for the Bridgeport Water Facility. I gave them a bargain."

"You mean you made drapes *like* these."

"No, I made these drapes."

"What are you talking about, Dad? Do you know where you are?"

"Stanley's Department Store," he answers confidently. Then he throws off his sheet and announces, "I have to pee."

I point to the catheter. "You don't have to get out of bed. You're all hooked up and ready to go."

"Okay." He's annoyed now, and more frenzied than before. "Let's go."

He begins to tug at the rubber hose. I get panicky, knowing he could hurt himself.

"Dad, you're in Hartford Hospital. You've had a fall."

He hears nothing, understands nothing, but keeps repeating, "Let's get out of here, okay? Okay? Okay?"

What's happening? I've never seen Dad this way before. Is he having another stroke?

"You're ruining me," he lashes out, bitterly. "Why won't you do the simplest thing I ask?"

He looks my way and sees a stranger. I feel eviscerated. His eyes are poisoned arrows, dipped in hate.

A Taste of Mortality
January 17, 2005

Dad is transferred by ambulance to the acute rehab unit at the Hebrew Home and Hospital, where a reassuring young doctor named Samuels takes me aside.

"I don't understand what's happening," I blurt out. "Dad's normally so sweet and easygoing. And compliant. It's eerie, seeing him like this."

"Your father is in a state of delirium," the doctor explains, finally giving a name to the gibberish coming out of Dad's mouth and the restless, fiery, psychotic look in his eyes. "It's actually very common among older patients—more than two million Americans suffer from it each year. Your dad's confusion could last a few more days, or longer. At his age, there are so many contributing factors—dehydration, an infection, a change in environment, sensory and sleep deprivation, drugs. We've stopped the morphine, but it's still in his system."

Dr. Samuels elaborates as though he has nothing but time and Dad is his only concern. How blessed we are to have a doctor who extends himself to his patients. The world could use more like him.

"If your dad were a young, healthy guy, he might have avoided this complication," he notes, "but his body is compromised."

The doctor pauses to take my emotional temperature, then says, "His condition is not benign."

Not benign? I've never heard the words used this way before.

"Does your father have health directives? He could die."

Die? Dr. Samuels could be talking about a cut or a bruise. I'm shocked into silence. I see an empty space where Dad once stood, and start to tremble, not for him, but for me.

TIME FLIES
January 18, 2005

Dad's mind clears, and he's happy to get out of bed and go for a stroll in a wheelchair. As I push him down the hallway, we pass the candy store manned by an elderly volunteer.

"How about a Hershey bar, Dad?" I ask rhetorically.

"That's good," he answers, brightening up.

"How many?"

"One." He pauses. "Two."

We charge the candy to his account, feeling as brash and buoyant as the owners of a new Ferrari. In the corridor, we bump into his physical therapist. "Mr. Lieff, today we're going to begin to teach you to eat with your left hand," he says, pointing cheerfully at Dad's sling.

"That's good," quips Dad, "because I want to get started on my Hershey bar."

Heading into Dad's room, I notice the name Sylvia Benton on the door across the hall. "No way," I hear myself saying. Sylvia and her husband, Roger—he died several years ago—were my parents' closest friends throughout my childhood. The couples even took a cruise together to South America. I vividly remember the photographs of them all partied up, wearing shiny tuxes and frilly cocktail dresses, smoking cigarettes, sipping martinis, fox-trotting the night away. It was in those pictures with the Bentons that my parents looked most lighthearted and alive.

Sylvia isn't in her room, so Dad and I go in search of her in the dining room. We find her slouched in a wheelchair, hooked up to an oxygen tank, looking pale and drawn. Could this be the gay, plucky girl I saw in the photos?

"Sylvia!" I call out. "Sylvia!"

Her eyes eventually find mine. "Hi. I'm Lou Lieff's daughter." I point to Dad. "Do you remember my dad, Lou? And my mother, Dolly?"

Sylvia nods, slowly returning to life. "Your mother was always so well-groomed," she says.

I worry that Dad will get depressed, trying to communicate with this ghost from the past, so I give her a hug and tell her we'll see her later.

Dad reaches out and takes her hand. "You look good," he says affectionately.

The truth is, she looks like hell, but maybe Dad feels good seeing her. Or maybe he just wants to cheer her up.

As I steer Dad away, Sylvia mumbles, "It's like a different world. Like a different world."

Time flies, as they say—whether you're having fun or not. Images of my parents and the Bentons race through my mind. So young, so old, so fast.

LIFE AND DEATH
January 19, 2005

Dad fell in the Hebrew Home rehab last night. How sick is that? I'm told he rolled forward in his wheelchair, headfirst onto the linoleum. It's a miracle he didn't break more bones, not that his aides are checking.

I call to cheer him up, but he's too weak to talk. After an uncomfortable silence, I hear him mumble, "I don't have the strength to hang up the phone."

Visiting him today, I'm struck by his ashen complexion, his shrunken cheeks. *Oh, God, this is how he'll look in the coffin.* It's the face of death. I see it for the first time.

The sequence of events startles me. Yesterday I crossed paths with Sylvia Benton. Then my niece Emily called to tell me she and her husband are expecting a baby this summer. She asked how her grandpa Louie is doing. Her other grandfather died a few weeks ago.

This is the natural order of things, the way it's supposed

to be. One generation steps down, the other steps forward with new life. I pause to think where I stand—am I coming or going?

A Day in the Madhouse
January 26, 2005

I find Dad in the hallway of the Hebrew Home, out cold in a reclining wheelchair. It's eleven in the morning, and he looks anesthetized.

"Would you give me an update on Dad?" I ask June, one of the many part-time nurses who rotate through the rehab unit.

She pulls his chart and flips through the pages. "He's on a diet of liquids and pureed food."

"Really?" I feel my head swell with anxiety. "Why is that?"

"He's having trouble swallowing."

"Really? When did that start?"

"I think he's been that way for a while," she says, a bit less confidently.

"No. He's always eaten well. Are you sure you have the right patient?'

June retreats behind the desk and checks the charts. When she returns, she says, "Actually, he's not on a liquid diet. He's on a no-sodium diet."

"Really? That's probably why he's so unhappy with the food. It tastes terrible. Why no sodium?"

"Because he has high blood pressure."

"No," I correct her. "He has low blood pressure. That's why we reduced his atenolol from 25 to 12/5 mg. His blood pressure was too low."

"Well," she asks, searching for an explanation, "does he have cardiac problems?"

My patience is thinning. "Fifteen years ago, he had triple bypass surgery."

"Oh." June lights up. "Maybe *that's* why he's on a sodium-free diet."

As she charges out of the room, I call out, "Please, change him back to normal food—today."

A few minutes later, another nurse comes in with a cup of pills. "Would you like them one-on-one or two-on-two?" she asks Dad. He looks up at me from his wheelchair as if to say, "Am I hearing right? Am I going crazy?"

Maybe those are my thoughts, not his.

The nurse asks Dad again, "Would you like your pills one-on-one or two-on-two?"

Silence. She turns to me. "Which would he like?"

I finally get it. "Dad, the nurse is asking you if you want one pill at a time or two at a time."

Dad throws me a look that says, "Who cares? I'm sick. I just want to get into bed."

"One at a time is fine," I tell the nurse. *Let it go. You can't control the universe.*

When June returns, I ask her for the results of Dad's

X-rays. She looks closely at his file and asserts unequivo-
cally, "The left shoulder is normal."

I want to kill her. "Yes, June, we know that. It's his right
shoulder we're worried about. That's why Dad is here—
because he broke his *right* humerus. Then he fell again on
his right side eight days ago—here, on the unit. Have you
gotten back the results?"

"No," she says blankly.

"June, I'd like to get the films today and send them to his
orthopedist. Can you help me?"

Things are starting to get bloody. The head nurse, alerted
by my shrill tone, steps in and says, "We can't release the
X-rays."

I try to reason with her. "If Dad needs to sign a form,
fine, but legally he owns his X-rays, not the hospital."

"That's right," she replies. "But they're not in this building."

I'm lost in the red tape, the bureaucratic web of paperwork and rules. Before I leave, I check the nurses' station
once more and find that the X-rays have been there all along,
but because they were taken by a low-level technician, when
Dad was in bed, they're fuzzy and unreliable.

Whatever. Time to quit. I head home. How Kafkaesque a
hospital experience can be. How scary to be old and aching
in such a maddening place, dependent on the judgment
and goodwill of part-time employees, many of them well-
intentioned but too overwhelmed to know their patients'
names, never mind their medical histories.

It's infuriating to be the caregiving child, trying to advocate for your parents and coordinate their care in an under-staffed, underpaid world.

It's exhausting to be a nurse or aide, saddled with too many patients who have too many problems and too many pushy relatives, like me.

It's a crucible of pain and frustration. For everyone.

GLUE PUDDING
February 13, 2005

"Try the dessert, Mr. Lieff," an aide at the Hebrew Home cajoles him. "You'll like it."

Dad struggles to hold a spoon in his left hand and lift his arm up to the table. I watch uncomfortably as the aide holds back help. It would be so much easier for everyone if she fed him, but the whole purpose of rehab is for Dad to be able to return to independent living, alone or with full-time assistance.

Dad eyes the sickly yellow glob on the tray in front of him. "It looks like glue," he proclaims.

"It's butterscotch pudding," the aide says with enthusiasm. "Try it!"

Dad brings the glutinous mass to his face and licks it.

"What do you think?" she asks gaily.

"Just as I thought," Dad replies, playing the game. "It *is* glue."

Another meal down the hatch. The aide laughs empathetically as she removes Dad's bib, rinses his face, and deposits him in his wheelchair in front of the TV. Dad just wants to get back into bed, but the nurses won't let him—they worry he'll develop pneumonia, spending so much time lying down.

Dad's life moves as slowly as glue these days. But I agree with him. It doesn't have to taste like glue.

The Empty Chair
March 13–15, 2005

Dad is back at Summerwood with full-time help. He can no longer be left alone. His tablemate Dave arrives at breakfast in slippers and announces that he has given up on socks. It can't be easy stretching the elastic and maneuvering your feet into narrow tubes when your hands shake from Parkinson's and your whole body loses its balance when you try to bend over.

The next time I see him, I hand him a pair with loose tops, the same ones I buy Dad from a department store for extra-large men. He lights up when he sees them. It isn't a big deal, but I light up, too, knowing I've made his life a little easier.

A few days later, Dave crashes to the ground, cracks his head on the pavement, and dies.

The morning of the funeral, Dad's physical therapist arrives at his apartment to do some shoulder exercises.

"Not today," Dad tells her.

I carpool the group, what is left of it—Dad, Murray, and Sam—to the mortuary. It's a poignant sight, the three old men bundled up in overcoats and wool hats and gloves, greeting the family before the service. Dad approaches Dave's son, who was married just two months ago. "How's your wife treating you?" Dad asks him, good-naturedly.

After a while we all move into the sanctuary for the funeral. The men have agreed not to go to the cemetery—they don't have the stamina to withstand the cold. There's also just so much death you can let into your life in a day.

The service ends around noon. While Dave's friends and family line up in their cars behind the hearse, I drive the men to lunch at the Elbow Room, one of their favorite restaurants in West Hartford Center, known for its giant burgers and sweet potato fries.

The guys sit around the wooden table in silence, chewing on their burgers, contemplating the changed composition of the group. Dad says out loud several times, "I can't believe this." Murray is uncharacteristically solemn. Sam, the one who doesn't get close to people easily, sits with his back turned to the fourth seat, now empty. "People come and go at Summerwood," he says. "I don't get too involved. I mind my own business."

Each processes the loss in his own way. And for three weeks, they don't allow another person to sit at their table and take Dave's place.

Like an Animal
April 3–4, 2005

"So, does my car need an oil change?" Dad asks on our drive home from the Crown.

He must see in my face that something's wrong. Dad gave his Camry to Joel five months ago.

"If you're mixed up, but you know you're mixed up, you can't be so mixed up," I joke, trying to keep things light. But since his bout of delirium, Dad seems more confused and vulnerable. I've hired a middle-aged Jamaican lady to live with him five days a week and coordinate coverage with her friends when she's not available.

"How are you getting along with Regina?" I ask.

"We fight."

"How come?"

"She hides the Ambien from me."

"Those are my instructions, Dad. You oversedate yourself, then you get out of bed and don't know where you are. You've fallen six times since you moved to Summerwood."

"She keeps the sides of the bed up," he says. "I hate that."

"I've told her to do that, too. If you want to get up at night, you have to ring the bell."

"She treats me like an animal."

"She doesn't want you to kill yourself. Neither do I."

"And she charges too much."

"The truth is, Pop, we couldn't pay her enough. You're no bargain. Someone else would have young kids at home, or a partner—or a life."

Dad grows quiet. I know Regina is not a perfect fit for him. She's too old, not in age but in spirit. Dad likes young, attractive girls with spunk, who make him feel alive. Regina is a good soul—pleasant, reliable, and devoted to Dad—but she's plodding and unambitious, content to sit in a chair all day. How boring it must be for the two of them to be confined to a tiny apartment, struggling to make conversation, searching for words to fill the spaces between them. Time must crawl by.

Where do my sympathies lie? Mostly with Regina, cooped up with a man who can't even remember her name. I cringe when I hear him speak to her: "Hey, can you bring me a glass of water?" "Miss, I need to use the bathroom."

This must be a nightmarish job, smearing cream on an old man's sores, wiping his tuchis, being summoned from sleep night after night by the insistence of a steel bell. What sustains her? Steady pay? The satisfaction of being put to use, caring for another? Her deep, abiding faith? Resentment must build on both sides. I'm sure Regina gets offended and lashes out in her own way.

I feel bad for Dad, too, reduced to infantile dependence, sitting in his steaming urine, being told what to do and when to do it. "Mr. Lieff," Regina gently chides him, "why didn't you tell me you had to go to the bathroom? I just changed you." What indignity. What humiliation. Who can fault him for striking back from time to time?

"I had sixty dollars by my bed," Dad tells me, as we near Summerwood. "Now it's gone."

"Look in your pocket."

Dad fumbles around in his pants and pulls out three crumpled twenty-dollar bills.

"They're killing me, these girls," he protests. "It's a disgrace how they treat me. Last night I had to beg them for a blanket."

"Dad, that was in the hospital, three months ago. It was very cold. You're comfortable now, aren't you?"

"Yes," he says, flustered, his eyes looking for a place to rest.

"Be here with me," I urge him gently. "Be here with me now."

I'm driving, but I reach over and stroke his tense muscles, his buttery skin, and then I stroke him some more, and for the time being he lets go of his terror and nods off to sleep.

The next day, on the phone, he repeats a familiar refrain: "She treats me like an animal."

"What's wrong?" I ask. "What's bothering you?"

Something incomprehensible pours out of his scrambled brain.

"Let me speak to Regina," I say.

A long silence, then Regina picks up the phone. "Your

father's unhappy because I make him push his walker in the hallway," she explains.

This is exactly what I want her to do: get him on his feet every few hours. Dad complains—he feels too weak. Should I leave the poor guy alone? Urge him to exert himself more? No one is right here.

"Regina," I say, "Dad is often confused these days. Please don't let his grumpiness get to you. He doesn't always know what he's saying. Can you pretend you're wearing headphones?"

"You tell your daddy it's okay. Jesus loves all his children." Regina laughs, and I'm relieved. The thought of her quitting makes me light-headed.

She hands the phone back to Dad.

"She's just doing her job, Pop," I say. "You can't just sit in the chair all day long, it's not good for you."

"Like an animal," Dad repeats.

I appeal to his sense of humor, trying a different tack. "Pop, I want you to stay calm. C-a-l-m."

I repeat the word softly, like a purring cat, trying to induce in him a peaceful state of mind.

"Yeah," he answers. "Like an animal."

Elder Abuse

"It's not easy, finding good help these days," a patient named Barbara complains. "My mother is still living in her condo but needs assistance around the clock. I manage

her care but rely on an agency to make sure she's covered 24/7. Aides come and go. Sometimes I call and someone picks up who doesn't know who I am, never mind how to reach me. It's terrible, abandoning Mom to strangers, but anything's better than an institution."

"I know you've worked hard to keep your mother at home."

"For the most part, the aides seem pretty nice and attentive. But it's scary to think what goes on when I'm not there. Mom says they're mean to her. The other day she told me she peed on the couch and the aide screamed at her, 'Next time, I'll make you clean it up yourself!' "

My heart goes out to Barbara and her mother. The elderly often imagine their caregivers are tyrannizing them, even when those caregivers are their own children. Their suspicions are often delusional, the result of a neuro-chemical imbalance or a psychological need to blame others for their own cognitive lapses. But there's no question, elder abuse is on the rise. A national survey of state adult protective services found more than a quarter million cases of elder abuse—emotional, verbal, physical, sexual, and financial. That's more than eight cases for every thousand older Americans. And because this mistreatment is often unreported or dismissed, it's likely to be just the tip of the iceberg.

"I'm tempted to report the aide but I have no hard evidence of abuse," Barbara tells me.

"You used an agency, you say? Have you shared your concerns with the manager? She might see a pattern of complaints against this particular aide. I'd also confront

*the aide yourself, and seriously weigh what she has to say.
The important thing is not to brush off your mother's accusations as the ramblings of a sick mind, but to honor
them and test their truth. You know her. Read between the
lines. So much of our suffering is done in silence. Someone old and defenseless may not recognize real danger, or
they may fabricate danger that doesn't exist."*

*"Sometimes I feel like a total fool, not knowing who to
believe," Barbara concedes. "I feel as unsure and confused
as my mother."*

*When Barbara leaves, I pick up the phone and call Dad's
buddy Sam. "Sam, I'd like your opinion on something.
Do you have a minute?"*

"Go ahead," he barks.

*"Dad has been complaining that the aides don't treat
him well. You have dinner with him every night. Have
you seen any evidence of abuse?"*

*"They're wonderful," Sam reassures me. "They keep
his clothes clean and treat him with respect. Summerwood
doesn't let them eat in the dining room, you know, but
they get him settled into his chair and stay long enough to
cut his food. They look out for him. Don't worry, I look
out for him, too."*

*I hang up and wonder, what goes on behind Dad's
door? Am I dismissing his complaints too glibly? If I am,
aren't I, for all my noble efforts to provide good care, par-
ticipating in his abuse?*

A Day in the Park
April 15, 2005

I watch Dad decline as quickly as an infant grows—one day crawling, the next day sprinting. Was it just a year ago I fought with him to turn in his cane for a walker? Skip ahead, and he prefers a wheelchair. Three months ago I wouldn't have embarrassed him by suggesting he wear Depends. Now I wouldn't embarrass him by taking them off.

Last week, I found Dad in his green chair, eyes vacant, mouth drooping, and rushed him to the hospital. "I'm bad," is all he could say. Fortunately, what looked like a stroke turned out to be nothing more than a urinary tract infection and gastric reflux, and he was transferred to the Hebrew Home for rehab.

Today, a glorious spring day, he greets me with a smile. I wheel him over to the playground next door and park him by the swings.

The sun beams down, and Dad immediately falls into a deep sleep. The children are fascinated by this big baby in a big stroller with big wheels. They seem to identify with him, get a kick out of him, delight in his presence. They are respectful, and even though they point at him and twirl around him, giggling, they know not to wake him.

Dad, eighty-five years old, napping in diapers. Once a man, twice a baby.

HUMAN TOUCH
April 30, 2005

Dad is ready to resume his life at Summerwood. As we drive through West Hartford Center, I see his dear friend Helen crossing the street.

"Helen!" I call out. "Helen!"

Helen is an attractive woman, well-preserved at eighty-two, a bit stout with large, supple breasts. Her silver gray hair looks natural and is always neatly coiffed. Helen is eminently approachable—a kind, gentle, practical caregiver who invites you in with an approving smile and radiant blue-green eyes. She and her husband, Alan, were good friends of my parents, and the level of affection ran high in all directions.

My mother died in 2000. Helen's husband died two years later. Dad, who usually shies away from sickness and disease, drove to their house to visit Alan on his deathbed. After the funeral, Helen told me, "It was so sweet of your father to spend the afternoon with Alan. When he left, Alan said to me, 'That's a very nice man.'"

I interpreted this to mean Alan wanted Helen to keep Dad as a friend when he was gone, and Helen wanted me to know. I was hoping that Dad and Helen would develop more than a friendship—not necessarily a sexual relationship, but an intimate bond. They wouldn't necessarily have to get married, although I couldn't imagine the two of them living together otherwise.

I could picture them leaning on each other, each providing resources the other lacked. Dad would make her smile and feel special. She would give Dad his medication and take him to the doctor. Dad would drive her to the movies (she doesn't drive) and the Crown Market. She'd cook him brisket in the winter and serve him cold borscht on hot days. Together they'd beat back the shadow of loneliness and fill the spaces in each other's hearts.

A few months later, Dad began to drive over to Helen's house on Mondays and take her to the senior center to play bridge. Helen began to invite Dad to come early for lunch. She'd make them sandwiches and pack some rugelach or brownies for him to take back to Summerwood. I noticed he was eating things with her that he never ate with Mom, like shrimp salad—food a little too rich for Mom's blood. This flirtation seemed strange to me. Good, but strange.

"I want to reciprocate," Dad told me one day. "Helen is always feeding me. But I can't cook. And I can't drive too far at night."

"How about inviting her to Summerwood?" I suggested. "It's an easy place to entertain. The food is decent, and it couldn't be more convenient."

I imagined Dad walking into the dining room with a woman—the attention it would stir.

A few weeks later, Dad told me, "Sam wants to invite

his sister to dinner. He said I should invite Helen, and the four of us could sit together. He says Friday night is a good time."

"That sounds great. You know how much I like Helen."

"You think she'd want to come?"

"Absolutely. You know, I always thought after Mom died you might hook up with Helen."

Dad laughed. "Ha. Who would want an old cocker like me?"

Dad had a point.

The evening unfolded, and the four of them had such a good time, they made it a regular monthly affair. Sam's sister, a retired elementary schoolteacher, would pick up Helen on her way to Summerwood, and Dad would drive Helen home at the end of the evening.

But as for Helen and Dad hooking up, or getting married, the timing of this courtship, it seems, just isn't going to work out. Dad's health is deteriorating fast, and he just isn't a viable candidate for any woman short of Florence Nightingale. Even before, he was too passive about trying to snag her—too shy or unsure or guilty to show a romantic interest in her. Of course, Helen could have made the first move if she were interested, which is the way it worked with my mother.

The circumstances for dating continue to fall apart. Sam's sister's arthritis has flared up, and she's now too ill to drive. Helen, unable to manage the upkeep of her home, has moved to an independent-living facility across town, and Dad has surrendered his car.

To this day, Dad and Helen remain very good friends, though most of their contact is by phone. Helen calls him at least once a week to check up on him, but visits are rare, and marriage out of the question.

"Helen! Helen!"

As I call out to her in West Hartford Center, Dad informs me, "She's deaf." This is an exaggeration, but not entirely.

I stop the car, run up to her, and put my arm through hers. Her face beams with delight when she sees that I'm with Dad. She comes over, reaches through the open window, and takes his hand. "Hi, Lou," she says warmly, caressing his tender flesh. Just like my mother. Just like his wife.

I watch Helen touch him and can feel the oxytocin fill his blood vessels. He must be starved for affection. All he has is Regina now, a hired hand whom he rings in the dark to hold his pee bottle. His days of cuddling with a lover are over.

We say good-bye to Helen, and I promise to call so we can all get together soon. As we drive away, I reach over and take Dad's hand.

I realize I'm a poor substitute for Helen, or Mom. I'm the dutiful daughter, the blood relative. And yet, who would deny the power and grace of human touch—one person reaching out to another, affirming the need we all share to have someone stroke our flagging skin, someone who declares, "You're good enough to love."

Replacing Mom

May 1, 2005

"It's disgusting, don't you think?" my friend Susan groans. "My poor mother's body is still warm in the grave, and Dad's dating this—gold digger. My mother never liked her. Would you believe, they're planning to buy an apartment in an independent-living facility."

"My father's peeing in a diaper," I point out, "and yours is having sex."

"Don't remind me. I don't want to think about it."

I try to console her. "I know it must upset you to see him replace your mother so quickly, but at least he's not alone and depressed, and there's less pressure on you to watch over him and keep him busy. Now he can bring his dirty laundry to *her*."

"Believe me, I know," she snickers. "But I've got to go. I'm off to make dinner. They're coming over tonight—with her daughter and grandchildren. We're just one big happy family. The whole thing is unreal."

I say nothing, but Susan's response strikes me as selfish and petty. "Your father has what I've wanted for mine," I'd like to tell her. "Someone to hold him at night and give him a reason to wash and shave. Not a daughter bound by blood or an aide paid to fill in, but a bona fide partner who would rather be with him than with anyone else. How great that he's grabbing on to life and holding on. Better than living alone with framed memories. . . . What difference does it make if he mourns for one month or ten, when he can't count on tomorrow? Why assume his loving another woman diminishes his love for your mother or defiles her memory? Love him enough to be happy for his happiness."

Back in my office, I'm drawn to a photo of my parents taken the year before Mom died. They're standing waist-deep in a swimming pool, smiling radiantly. A wide-brimmed straw hat keeps the sun off Dad's nose, once afflicted with skin cancer. Dark sunglasses, direct from the flea market, protect their eyes, clouded by cataracts. Mom's hand reaches across her belly and rests comfortably on his. The diamond ring they worked so hard to afford glitters on her finger. Dad's arm is wrapped around her waist, drawing her in. I can feel them touching each other.

If Dad took on a new partner—an Evelyn or a Helen—would I really feel relieved to hand over the burden of caring? Or would I feel replaced? My response, like Susan's, would likely be complicated, layered. A daughter spends a lifetime competing with her mother for her father's love. What if she lost him to a stranger? She'd have to accept that this person who raised her was not just her father but an individual with needs of his own. What would a glut of new relatives do to her nuclear family? And what if her father began to transfer not only his affection, but also his assets—

her inheritance—to this woman? To her children and grandchildren? Would she feel robbed and betrayed?

I'll never know what it would be like for Dad to take a
new bride. These days, his chances of enjoying young love
are as great as his hitting another hole in one. I complain
about Dad's dependence on me, the hard, thankless work,
but there's another part of me that likes being the center of
his life. I'm not planning to give up the job, and it doesn't
seem likely that Dad is going to join JDate anytime soon.

A Sense of Humor
May 7, 2005

One good thing about having a sense of humor is that it
doesn't require a full set of dentures or thick hair. You can
be old and frail—and very funny. Dad's mind these days
usually doesn't work fast enough to remember a punch line,
but he still loves to entertain and be entertained.

We're sitting on the open porch at Summerwood, passing
time, when we overhear Maurice and Rose ribbing each other.
Maurice, the new man at Dad's table, isn't taking Dave's place
so much as occupying it. Already he's pushing to make a
shiddach—a match—with this seventy-nine-year-old widow.

"I went to the Hebrew Home and bought flowers at a
fund-raiser there," Maurice boasts. "I'm philanthropic."

"Really," Rose answers, eyes twinkling. "I thought you were Jewish."

We all cackle. Maurice reaches over and takes Rose's liver-spotted hand. Other residents pull up a chair on this lovely May day, dressed against the chill. Muriel jumps in with her joke. "My son told me this one yesterday," she says. "Let's see if I can remember it: Two little girls are playing together. One says, 'You know, Mommy was very angry at Daddy last night. She said she found a condom on the patio.' 'Really?' the other says. 'What's a patio?'"

Once again, the group giggles. They may be impotent and incontinent, but they still know how to have a good time, to be silly, to be young at heart. They inspire me. There are many ways to rage against the dying of the light.

Karma
May 24, 2005

"Mr. Lieff, can you take a few steps for me?"

The radiologist, Judith Buckley, takes Dad's hand and helps him up. He shuffles forward a few inches, then, with a plaintive, "please-rescue-me" look, collapses back into his chair.

Dad's prostate cancer howls through his bones. He spends most of his waking hours popping painkillers, propped up in his big green chair or stretched out in bed. I'm praying Dr. Buckley can relieve his misery.

She leads me into her private office and closes the door. "I know what you're going through," she says, fixing me in her warm, intelligent gaze. "I've been there with my father. You don't want the treatment to be worse than the disease. I promise I won't let that happen."

I wonder whether her father is still alive, but steer the conversation back to myself. "My son Aaron is getting married in July," I say. "What wouldn't I give to have Dad there."

"Let's start with a shot of Quadramet. It should cut his pain so he can be more active. We don't want him wasting away in a wheelchair. As for the wedding, I don't know that he'll dance the hora, but I can see him—how do you say it?—kvelling from the sidelines."

As I get up to leave, she hands me her cell phone number. "Call anytime," she says.

I'm floored by her generosity. Some radiologists are more comfortable with images than with people, but not Dr. Buckley. If the world were ruled by feelings, I'd give her a big hug.

Next stop, the radiology department at Hartford Hospital for yet more tests. We're waiting in a cramped office when a young male technician comes stalking in. His streaked blond hair is cropped close to his scalp, and a diamond stud radiates from his left earlobe.

"You're scheduled for an X-ray, is that right?" he asks, staring down into his clipboard. He seems hassled, preoccupied, high-strung.

"Yes, and I believe a brain scan."

"It's not authorized."

"We just came from seeing Dr. Buckley. She ordered these tests."

"Dr. Buckley knows you can't get a brain scan here."

Why, I wonder, is someone so wounded working in a cancer clinic, preying on the frailties of the sick and dying? I want to decimate him, but let my fury pass. Maybe his father died of cancer. Maybe *he* has cancer.

Several phone calls later, everything is straightened out, and Dad takes his tests. I drop him off at Summerwood and head back to Westport. My office phone is ringing as I open the door. It's a woman named Eileen, pleading to come in for a session. I can hear the scream in her voice. Her husband, she just learned, is having an affair. I have a thousand things to do, but I let Eileen talk through her despair, and respond as patiently and sympathetically as I can. She doesn't know Dr. Buckley or the hospital technician, but they are standing here beside me, informing my response. Maybe tomorrow Eileen will show an extra bit of kindness to someone else in need.

Call it karma: one person caring for another. Pass it on.

OCD

June 3, 2005

Emergencies are now the norm. The unexpected is familiar. When the phone rings, I'm gripped by a sense of inevitability. It's Nikia, Dad's new twenty-one-year-old Jamaican aide who, despite her spangled nails and colored braids, seems as sensible as a towel.

"Your dad fell. He was holding on to his walker and just keeled over backward. We're in the ambulance, on the way to the hospital."

"I'll meet you there."

Dad is scheduled for his first dose of Quadramet today. Instead of canceling, Dr. Buckley rushes over to the emergency room to give him his shot. More good news: nothing is broken. Dad is having trouble standing, but neurologically he's "fine." I drop him and Nikia off at Summerwood, then drive north to Springfield for the grueling, all-day workshop I'm giving tomorrow. I'm in bed reading when the phone rings. It's Nikia.

"Your dad is having chest pains and wants to go to the hospital."

Let's all check in.

"Ask him, on a scale of one to ten, how bad they are."

A pause. "Eight, he says."

Should I send them back to the hospital? We can't run there every day. Actually, we could. We could. But I don't have the heart to send Nikia back, and what if I do and she quits?

"Give him two Tums and see how he is in an hour," is the best I can come up with. It's a remedy that has worked before. But I could be dead wrong.

Time to sleep. I fold back the page of my book: 288—a magical number for me, weighted with memories.

The past springs open like the door of a safe. I'm eight or nine, and in my parents' house in West Hartford. We're in the den, as we are every night after dinner, arranged around a black-and-white TV—Dad sunk in his black leather La-Z-Boy recliner, Mom stretched out on the nubby beige couch beside him, Joel and I sprawled on the shaggy brown carpet in a sea of foam-filled pillows.

Mom serves up chunks of fresh fruit and hot decaf tea with a squeeze of lemon. We let her wait on us.

All's well with the world. But then Dad gets quiet. "Labe, are you sick?" Mom asks.

Dad's face is glazed in sweat.

"Are you having chest pains? Do you want me to call the doctor? Do you want to go to the emergency room? Do you need your nitroglycerin?"

Some days Dad is fine. Not today. "Come on, let's go," Mom says, madly scrambling to load him in the car. Dad is doubled over. I can't bear to look at him. I think he's crying. The garage door rattles open. Tires screech. The emergency room is fifteen minutes, a lifetime, away. I sit immobilized in the den, wide-eyed, heart pounding. Joel, three years my elder, is the designated babysitter. He sits staring at the flickering tube, as though his life depends on it. What are we watching? *Dr. Kildare?* I slink off to my room, bolt the door, and begin bargaining with God. "I'll be good," I promise. "I'll be so good. Please, God, save Dad tonight. I'll never ask for anything ever again. Bring him home one more time."

The next day, Dad came back. He always did. And I developed a psychological disorder called OCD—obsessive-compulsive disorder. In my mind, I owned the power to rescue him from death. The rules were clear. Every night, before I went to bed, no matter how sleepy, no matter how exhausted, I was required to line up my dolls and stuffed animals around the perimeter of my room and call out their names, left to right: *Sammy. Petunia. Mickey. Roadrunner. Teeny Beeny. Rhonda. George.* So long as I kept my side of the bargain, Dad was safe.

I was also not permitted to stop reading on a page with a two or an eight in the number—my birthday was 8/28, August 28. If I could continue to a "safe" page, Dad would live, at least for another day. I knew consciously that his fate was beyond my control, that I had no magical gifts, but whenever I dared to stop reading on a page with a two or eight, a voice in my head would warn me—the same voice my mother used when I misbehaved—"You're going to kill your father." So I'd go back to my book and read some more.

Eventually, Dad had triple bypass surgery, and his chest pains disappeared, but emotional scars remained for all of us.

I gaze down at page 288. Is it possible that after half a century I'm still shadowed by this stupid superstition? If I don't turn the page, will Dad die tonight? Should I take a chance?

"Turn off the light, Jan," I instruct myself. "Just turn it off and put the book down. Go to sleep."

I try, but I can't stop the buzzing in my head, the imminent sense of threat, the crazy, compulsive urge to read just one more page. *It's comforting to think you can control the universe, Jan, but face it: you're as powerless today as you were as a child.*

I gulp down five milligrams of Ambien. It does nothing for me. I take another and succumb to sleep.

THE FIGHT
June 11, 2005

Dad's health has stabilized, thanks to the Quadramet injections. He seems pretty chipper these days and can get around with his walker again. His gastric reflux problem also has improved: an assortment of physical therapists have observed him swallowing and say he's fine, so long as he chews his food slowly and sips lots of water between bites. What better place to celebrate than at his favorite burger joint, the Elbow Room?

Dad is chewing away the afternoon when Michael announces he's languishing for ice cream, and heads down the street to Maggie Moo's for a chocolate cone. We wait for him forever.

"Where were you?" I grouse, when he finally returns.

"Where were *you*?" he snaps back. "We were supposed to meet at the car."

"Never."

"I didn't just make it up."

We drive Dad back to Summerwood in silence. "So, Dad," I say, fumbling for words to diffuse the tension, "I think Summerwood is showing a good movie tonight."

Dad sits pensively, privy to the unspoken truth. Michael and I drop him off and spend the drive home processing what happened.

"You need to be clearer next time."

"You need to listen better."

"You shouldn't wander off in the middle of lunch."

"I have restless legs. I didn't mean to keep you waiting."

We apologize grudgingly to each other, both of us feeling wronged, both of us knowing we've made too much of it, and all is fine—except I feel terrible for Dad. What's the point of treating him to a great meal when all he wants is to see his kids happy? I call him as soon as I get home.

"You may have noticed that Michael and I weren't getting along," I admit sheepishly.

"Why are you two fighting?" he asks, perturbed. "What could be so important?"

"We talked it out. Don't worry. We're fine."

"That's good."

I feel rotten, having spoiled Dad's day, and vow to stay

true to my purpose when I visit him in the future. I also vow not to fight with Michael over stupid things, a vow I know I'll never keep. Watching Dad's decline reminds me of the obvious, that life passes quickly and we shouldn't squander precious time. Petulance is the prerogative of the strong and healthy, those in denial of death.

SHORT-TERM MEMORY LOSS
July 16, 2005

I ring Dad to hear how he's doing. "He was really shaky this morning," Nikia reports, "so I brought his breakfast upstairs to his room."

The caregivers have begun to feed Dad in his apartment when they feel he isn't cogent enough to sit at the men's table in the dining room and be good company. They're protecting his dignity and status at Summerwood, and guarding him against personal embarrassment. One of the residents complained recently that Dad makes a mess when he eats. Nobody wants to have dinner with someone who's out to lunch.

Dad takes the receiver. He sounds rattled. His speech is racing. "So are we all set for the wedding . . . ?" He stops. "Wait. I'm confused. What am I saying?"

I pause and speak to him delicately. "Dad, the wedding was two weeks ago. Nikia and her mother drove you up to

Vermont, remember? Aaron helped you with your tie, the same one he was wearing. And you rode a golf cart across the lawn to the chuppah."

"Of course!" he exclaims.

"And you asked me how big a check you should give him, and I said, 'How about a thousand?' and you said, 'That sounds right because it's about twice what I was thinking.'"

"Ha." Dad chuckles. "Did I say that?"

"It was so great that you were there. That was the best gift of all."

Dad grows quiet again.

"You're mixed up today," I say, trying to sound upbeat.

"I am," he acknowledges. Then, perking up, he adds, "Go for a swim!" I interpret this to mean, "Don't worry about me. Do something for yourself. Have fun."

I take his counsel and begin to unwind, knowing he's back on this planet, at least for today.

THE CARETAKER
July 27, 2005

Since most of Dad's falls take place at night, I've instructed him, begged him, to ring his bell for help and not get up by himself. He obliges, except when he doesn't, and then he often stumbles and crashes to the ground.

In trying to solve this problem, I create another: his bell

wakes up the caregiver in the apartment below. She complained to management this morning and gave Dad's weekend aide, Portia, a piece of her mind outside the dining room. Portia is no pussycat herself, and the two of them got into quite a verbal brawl.

"We can't have this kind of disturbance from the aides," the director of Summerwood warns me, with a mix of disapproval and compassion. She knows I'm left to deal with the fallout.

"What exactly happened?" I ask.

"I wasn't there, but I hear that Portia called the aide an African cunt."

"I'll talk to her," I groan. "Maybe I can get Dad an intercom system."

I spend my days caught in the cross fire of my patients; now I have to manage the help I've hired to make my life easier. I resent Portia's indiscretion, the extra work she's causing me, and I begin to think about replacing her. She's the weakest link in the chain of people who care for Dad. Lately, she seems whiny, lethargic, and absentminded.

"Portia, what happened?" I ask, bracing myself for her version of the truth.

"That woman in the downstairs apartment is a real bitch. Mr. Lieff has to use the bell to call me. Is he supposed to break his neck so she can sleep?"

"I appreciate your wanting to keep Dad safe," I say, trying to contain my frustration, "but you can't fight with the other workers, no matter how they provoke you. If you have a problem with anyone at Summerwood, please, from now on, tell me, and I'll handle it. Okay?"

She nods reluctantly.

"Two other things. I call sometimes and you're not here. Other times, you have your boyfriend over. It makes Dad uncomfortable."

"Janis," she counters, "I'm with your father sometimes three days in a row. I step out for a smoke or to do the wash. My boyfriend stopped by because your dad wanted pizza for lunch. He brought some over."

"Portia, I understand you must feel caged at times. I just ask you to realize that when Dad's left alone, he's likely to try to get up by himself, and that's just asking for trouble.

"I know you take very good care of him," I add, hoping to inspire her to do better.

I head home, and call to check in just before Dad takes his Ambien and signs off for the night. The phone rings and rings. Finally, Dad picks up.

"Hi, Pop, you getting ready for bed?"

"Yeah. But the girl's sound asleep."

"What? Put Portia on the phone."

"Portia," I hear him calling out. "Portia! Portia!"

"This is unbelievable. Dad, hang up the phone. I'll call back. Let it ring until it wakes her up."

I phone again, but Portia is out cold. Finally, Dad picks up again.

"Hi, Sher."

"Dad, I don't want you to move. Do you hear me? I'm

going to call downstairs to the front desk and have the night staff come to your apartment and wake Portia up."

Portia grabs the phone. "I just dozed off. I'm sorry, Janis."

I'm not sympathetic. "Portia, this just can't happen. Are you all right?"

I worry about her taking drugs and failing to respond to Dad. I worry about Dad being too drugged to call her. I worry about the aide downstairs hearing his calls for help and getting him kicked out of Summerwood.

This is not my definition of help. But where did I get the idea that aides come conflict-free? Portia isn't mean-spirited, she's just young—twenty-one. Dad is just a job. She's no more interested in caring for him than in waiting on tables. The truth is, I'm no more interested in her than she is in me, or Dad.

Fortunately for all of us, Portia quits the next day. I learn soon after that she has gotten a job working in a travel agency, answering phones. Perhaps she's dreaming of some faraway place that will relieve her of her boredom, some romantic hideaway where she can party all night with her well-toned boyfriend, not tend to an old geezer like Dad.

ROME, SHMOME
August 1, 2005

It's 1967. I'm sixteen, and Dad is driving me to the Boston area to check out a couple of colleges.

The Wellesley interview is a bust. The admissions director wants to know how many times I've been to Europe. "I've never been farther than Miami Beach," I apologize.

"How many times have your parents been to Europe?"

"They took a cruise once to Venezuela."

I leave, feeling unworthy, defeated, outclassed.

Next comes Brandeis, in Waltham. As we approach the campus, Dad stops at a deli for some sandwiches, then pulls over along a riverbank. "Come on," he calls out. "Let's go fishing. We're early."

I'm not sure what's on his mind, but I'm in too big a funk to care. He opens the trunk and takes out a frayed blanket and two beat-up fishing rods. We hook plastic worms on our lines and cast them into the water. "Sit down and take it easy," Dad says. And so we do, for most of an hour, chomping on our sandwiches, starring out into the river, lulled by the gentle current and warm breeze.

Eventually, we pack ourselves up, get back in the car, and head to the Brandeis admissions office. I feel better—still nervous, but less unglued.

That was thirty-odd years ago. I don't remember whether we hooked a trout or a clump of weeds—probably neither. But I know I soared through the interview, thanks in no small measure to Dad, who applied a healing balm to his disabled daughter and helped her stay calm and centered.

Dad steadied me again years later, when I was dating Michael and he flew off to Rome alone to research a book on early Christian martyrs. I couldn't go anyway—I was taking my kids skiing out west—but I was unhinged.

"Why does he have to go to Rome without me?" I whined. "Of all places, I love Rome the most."

"Rome, shmome," Dad said, hooking me with a smile. "What's so great about Rome?"

He was right. Sometimes things turn out the way we want. Sometimes they don't. We decide how miserable we want to be.

Even now, with death in the wings, I can hear Dad say, "Rome, shmome."

Compassion Fatigue
August 11, 2005

I grab the phone. It's Nikia. She took Dad on the Summerwood van to see *March of the Penguins* last night, and as the opening credits rolled across the screen, he lapsed into a state of delirium. The two of them were whisked back to his apartment. I didn't expect the calm to last, but neither did I expect the storm to come again so soon.

I page Dad's urologist and reach a stranger on call. "What did you say your father's name is?" he asks. "Would you spell it for me?"

I could take Dad to the emergency room, the doctor suggests. He could also prescribe an antibiotic, but the pharmacy is miles away and doesn't deliver until noon, and Nikia can't drive. Checkmate.

"Give him plenty of fluids and call me in a couple of hours," I tell Nikia guiltily. "Let's see how he does."

The truth is, I don't want to change my plans. Several weeks ago, in a fit of self-indulgence, I invited two out-of-town college roommates for lunch today. Everything is set.

As luck would have it, Dad feels better after breakfast, and the day is saved. My friends arrive, and we arrange ourselves around the pool. Dipping asparagus spears in sesame hummus, we catch up on each other's lives: one of them is going to see *A Moon for the Misbegotten* next week, for the second time, after a Velázquez show at the Met. The other swears by her new yoga teacher, and by a splashy new restaurant in Hartford with a seafood fra diablo to die for.

I'm on the phone every hour, calling Nikia to check on Dad's progress. I love my friends and am grateful for their company, but by two I wish they would go—I have too much on my mind. They're in no rush, however. Neither has a job, and neither has to be anywhere else. They have all the time in the world.

I'm jealous. They seem so free, so open to possibilities, so available for whatever comes next. Their parents are gone. I don't wish Dad dead, I just want to be rid of my obligation to him. *I want my life back.* This pummeling, day after day, this constant state of high alert, feels not simply burdensome but punishing. Like an affliction. A curse I can't shake off. And Dad doesn't even live with me. And he isn't even demanding.

Sipping iced cappuccinos, my friends ask me what I'm reading. I recite a passage from Kundera's *The Unbearable*

Lightness of Being: "There is nothing heavier than compassion. Not even one's own pain is as heavy as the pain one feels with someone, for someone—a pain intensified by the imagination and prolonged by a hundred echoes."

My friends tell me it's time to leave.

There's a psychological term for the burnout I feel. It's called "compassion fatigue." With no relief in sight, with too much responsibility and too little control, caregivers absorb their patients' trauma and become what Robert Butler calls "the second patient." Depleted by the chronic stress of serving others, they develop headaches, they can't sleep, they feel generally irritable, preoccupied, depressed. They stop taking care of themselves, substituting drugs and food for what they need most—exercise, nurturing relationships, good times. They start to have accidents.

I fit the bill. In the past year, I've had three collisions talking on my cell phone, trying to coordinate Dad's care when I should have been watching the road.

It's all too much. I'm supposed to be Dad's life preserver, but I'm the one who's drowning. I should see a psychologist. I should call myself up and make an appointment.

Meryl

"My mother died last month, two days short of eighty,"
a nervous, middle-aged patient named Meryl tells me.
"Everything was wrong with her—diabetes, heart dis-

ease, cataracts, you name it. Friends still keep coming up to me to express their condolences—'Oh, I'm so sorry to hear about your mom,' they say. 'It's so hard to lose a parent.' They look at me with sad, imploring eyes, press my hand, rub my back, give me a solemn hug. My problem is, I'm not sad. Is that terrible to say? I'm not only not sad, I'm relieved. My mother was a cranky, demanding woman. No love has been lost here. So when my friends ask me, 'How are you doing?' I want to say, 'I'm doing fine, thank you. I nursed Mom through the last twelve years of her life, and now that this crippling burden is off my shoulders—now, while there's still time and my husband and I still have our health—all I want to do is play golf. Call me a sick, selfish bitch—this is who I am.'"

"I'm not here to judge you," I reassure her. "Even if your mother was the sweetest, most easygoing person in the world, you might have experienced some relief when she died. Caring for an elderly parent is so invasive, so draining—it seems unfair to condemn yourself for wanting your life back.

"I also wouldn't be too hard on your friends for offering their condolences. They may be doing nothing more than trying to lighten your burden and telling you what they think you want to hear. If they could read your heart, they might admit that they, too, were dealt an escape-from-prison card when their parents died.

"Meryl, your mother was such a major presence in your life. For years, you bowed to her will and her ways. Now she's gone, and you're anxious to reclaim your life. You hold the keys. Your freedom is in your hands."

Diaper Dependence
August 20, 2005

Time for lunch, one of the few activities Dad and I can still enjoy together—although even this is a challenge. I load Dad and his wheelchair into the car, and head over to a new Thai restaurant at a local mall.

We stick to familiar dishes—chicken soup with noodles, shrimp with broccoli. I do my best to spoon-feed Dad, but his chin is so low against his chest, I can barely find his mouth. He struggles to swallow, defying gravity. When we finish, I mop up the mess and excuse myself to go to the bathroom. On my return, Dad announces that he has to go, too.

Fair enough, but how do you lift a 170-pound man who can hardly stand? I see him crashing on the tile floor or peeing all over his pants.

"Dad," I say guiltily, "I'm afraid I'll drop you. Could you go in your Depends?"

How easy. How awful. It's hard enough being swaddled in a diaper, but to sit in one, soaked in urine?

"I hate asking you to do this. Does it feel gross?"

"When I pee in a diaper?" he asks, without shame. "At first it feels wet and warm, but then the pee gets absorbed."

I look at him blankly. I can't be having this conversation with a grown man, my father.

My heart goes out to him. He's such a good sport. But my God, the indignities of old age.

THE LANGUAGE OF LOVE
August 26, 2005

Usually when I tell Dad I love him, he replies, "That's good." I feel love between the lines, in the warmth of his tone, in his smiling eyes, but these aren't the words I want to hear.

Today, though, as I kiss him good-bye and say, "I love you," he startles me and says, "I love you, too."

Curiously, I don't feel reassured or comforted. I hear words spoken when time is running out, as though a voice is telling him, *You had better speak up now because there may be no tomorrow.* I hear the end approaching.

SILENCE IS GOLDEN
September 7, 2005

Dad has always been a man of few words, but lately he seems to have shut down completely. I don't know why this unsettles me so, why I can't just sit in silence with him, and let him be.

I ask him a question and barely wait for a response before I blabber on. Does he not have the energy to talk? Maybe his brain is too jumbled for him to retain what I'm saying and comment back. If I gave him more time, would he answer?

Dad may be content just sitting still and letting the world spin around him, but sometimes I just have to know what he's thinking. I can't help myself.

"What's on your mind?" I ask, point-blank. He answers with a look that says, "What's there to say?"

I wonder whether Dad says nothing simply because he hates to complain. If he gave voice to his feelings, would he tell me, "I miss your mother," or "I hate this place," or "I feel sick as hell"? What I get instead is a serene Buddha smile.

There are times when I want to ask him penetrating questions that tap his deepest thoughts. I want to know him better. I want to ask, "How is your life, really?" "Do you think about dying?" "Do you have any regrets?" "Do you have any advice for me?" But I don't want to upset him or force my agenda on him, so I say nothing, or I say a lot, and nothing at all.

Today's outing takes us to the rose garden in Elizabeth Park, our favorite retreat. The weather is gorgeous—bright, comfortably warm, with a scent of fall in the air.

Dad sits restfully.

"I love those wild grasses," I say fervently, pointing to them, "but my neighbor Beth says they attracts snakes. She's got them around her pool."

Dad says nothing.

"What a day! How great to be outdoors!"

I sound so ridiculous. I'm embarrassed to be in my company. My chatter makes my skin crawl.

I set Dad up on his favorite bench under an expansive oak, facing some red and yellow roses fading on their wasted stems. I place a can of Stewart's diet root beer on a TV snack table in front of him, and wrap his tremulous hands around half a tuna fish sandwich from the Crown.

When the bees arrive, I park another can on the ground a few yards from our site. "Let's give the bees their own picnic," I say.

A few minutes pass. We listen to the distant buzzing.

Dad eats, bite by excruciating bite.

"Want to take a walk?" I finally ask, breaking the silence.

Dad doesn't say no, so I pack up what's left and wheel him along a paved path through the garden. We find the pond and park there for a few minutes to watch the ducks splash and peck and paddle.

Why, I wonder, must I entertain to be of value, wearing out my audience and myself in the process? Isn't it enough, really, to be alive, to be together in the world, all senses intact? Can't silence be just as intimate as talk? Can't we touch sometimes without words?

I'm edgy. I have too much going on at work and in my head to lend myself to the moment. The roses, the sky, the visit—all add to my anxiety.

I look at my watch. I have to be on the road in an hour.

"How about an ice cream?" I propose.

We drive off, and Dad falls into a deep sleep. I imagine I've exhausted him—I know I've exhausted myself. Maybe he's just being kind, giving me a reprieve from him.

One strawberry cone later, I deposit Dad in his apartment and help Nikia prepare him for his afternoon nap.

"Thank you for a lovely day," he says, with total earnestness, before nodding off. His words shake me. He has had a lovely day just being outdoors, getting away from Summerwood and hanging out with the bees and the ducks and the roses. Because of me. In spite of me.

TILLIE
September 8, 2005

How is it that some people can talk so openly, so matter-of-factly, about death, while others remain resolutely silent, as though death were not for the living? Why do we keep something so inevitable and banal locked up inside us?

This morning, my friend's mother, Tillie, told her doctor to remove the tube from her lung. "I've lived a wonderful life," she said, "and I'm ready to go." Then she told her son, "Let's talk about the funeral. I don't want to be buried in a chicken crate, like your father. That's fine for an Orthodox Jew, but I want something more comfortable, more plush. Do you remember the violinist who played at Aunt Ethel's funeral? She could play Yiddish lullabies at mine. I want people to have a good time."

Now there's one fearless woman. Dad never, ever mentions death. Is he afraid to peer over the edge? Perhaps he labors under some primitive belief that by talking about the end, he brings it nearer—that what he doesn't articulate won't happen. Perhaps he just wants to avoid unpleasant table talk.

And me, I avoid discussing death with Dad as religiously as he does. It should be simple enough to ask him, "Dad, do you have instructions for me when you die?" But I don't go there, either.

I should. The time to explore Dad's preferences is now, while his mind is still intact and death is something that happens to others. But I hesitate.

I hesitate.

Is it that I don't want to shove Dad's mortality in his face and frighten him with my tears? Or is it his tears I can't bear to see?

How sad, how ironic it would be if I were deferring to what I think are his wishes, and he, not wanting to make me squirm, were deferring to what he thinks are mine.

I wish Dad would direct me, but if he did, he wouldn't be Dad.

And so I wait, as if I know when the bell will toll.

ANOTHER DAY, ANOTHER CRISIS
September 23–24, 2005

Dad seems to be on a quick downward slide. Over the past two months he has developed an ugly, cancerous tumor on his ear and begun to gag on food. There's no hiding from it: Dad has begun to die. I don't mean the kind of dying that begins the day we're born, but the kind that signals the end of life.

On my way to Boston to give an all-day course on forgiveness, I stop at Dad's apartment and find him slumped in his recliner. "The poppa! The poppa!" I sing out, with my usual over-the-top enthusiasm. He smiles wanly. When he speaks, a gurgling sound bubbles up from his throat.

"Are you having trouble breathing?" I ask.

"No."

"Are you sure?"

"Yes."

I turn to Nikia. "What do you think?"

"He's not right. I think we should go to the emergency room."

I can't. We'll be there all day, waiting to be seen, taking tests. I have a talk to give.

Buying time, I unpack my weekly offering: Eskimo Pies, watermelon spears, an inexpensive bottle of Merlot. *Is he still drinking wine, with all the medication he's taking?* I hold up a steaming container of matzo ball soup from the Crown.

"Want some?"

"Sure," he says, weakly.

I feed him a few spoonfuls as the clock pushes forward. He slurps and coughs, slurps and coughs.

"Okay," I tell Nikia. "Let's go." I call the ENT specialist we're scheduled to see next week and leave a message that we're on our way to the emergency room. Could he stop by? *What are the chances of that?*

I wheel Dad into the hospital and give the admitting nurse his name. "There's nothing acutely wrong with him," I apologize. "He doesn't have a fever or infection that I can see, but he seems slow and raspy."

She looks Dad over. "It's amazing how some people run here every time they get a cough or runny nose, while others, the really sick ones, stay home. Your dad is where he belongs."

We're ushered into a private room. Two male aides, dressed in hospital green, step in, pushing an enormous aluminum contraption. "Walter?" they call out.

I panic. "No, this is Louis Lieff. Whatever you're planning to do, stop!"

I imagine Dad having a kidney removed or a leg amputated because he's taken for Walter. You have to be mad to come to an emergency room without an advocate.

I look at my watch. *How can I leave? How can I not go?*

I have a long drive and a long day ahead of me tomorrow, and give myself permission to take off. Nikia agrees to stay. We'll keep in touch by phone.

The next day I survive my six-hour workshop, calling Nikia for an update at every break. It's an endless ride home after an exhausting presentation, and for a second my eyes close and I catch myself swerving off the road. The hospital exit is fast approaching—should I check on Dad? It's the last thing I want to do.

I veer onto the ramp and head for the emergency room.

Just run in and see that he's okay.

It's rush hour. Traffic creeps through the city. Another voice rescues me: *You've done enough today. Take care of yourself. Go home.*

I pull into a McDonald's for a chocolate sundae to go. Now I really feel shitty.

Back on the highway, I call Dad. Nikia answers: "Your father wants to speak to you." He takes forever, fitting the receiver to his ear. Then he wheezes, "I'm in the hospital, I have pneumonia"—as though we haven't talked for years.

"I'll call you often, Dad," I promise. "Any time you want to talk, just ask Nikia to call me."

"It's hard," he answers. "It's hard."

I feel like a car running on empty, with nowhere to fill up.

Nikia takes the phone back. "Your dad always perks up when he hears your voice," she says, reinforcing my sense of culpability.

I pick up speed. When it comes to taking care of a sick,

aging parent, you can never do enough. You can't ever do enough for yourself either, and your guilt knows no bounds.

THE J-TUBE
September 25, 2005

An upper GI barium test reveals that Dad can't swallow effectively—not food, not even his own saliva. That's how he developed pneumonia in the first place. Liquids leaked into his lungs.

Dad is taken off water, food, and medication to prevent choking. His sole source of nourishment is an IV sugar drip—not enough to live on, just enough to sustain him for a week or two while we decide what to do next.

The ENT doctor never shows up or calls. Another one delivers the ominous news: Dad needs a feeding tube to survive. His tuna fish and root beer days are over.

The J-tube, as it's called, would be surgically inserted through an opening in his stomach and anchored to his small intestine. Breakfast? A liquid mix of protein, fiber, and carbohydrates—all kosher, thank you—poured into his body. Lunch and dinner? The same. Dad might experience some pain, burning, and constipation from time to time, but the tube would be securely lodged inside him, and he wouldn't be confined to bed.

I try to imagine life with a J-tube. No chewing, licking, sipping, or swallowing. No tastes or smells, except your own.

"Could Dad eat ice cream?" I ask the doctor. "He loves ice cream."

"Probably not. Ice cream is hard when it's frozen, but it quickly dissolves and he wouldn't be able to handle the liquid. His brain wouldn't have enough time to adjust to the change."

"So, no water?"

"No water."

This is unfathomable to me, but I go on.

"What about soup, like clam chowder? He loves clam chowder."

"Maybe, if it's mixed with a thickener, and then all the ingredients are blended together."

Focusing on clam chowder takes my mind off the larger existential issue: at what point is a life not a life? And who decides? I am Dad's health-care proxy, his voice, his protector. He gave me that right. But who am I to judge that he has had enough life, that life for him is no longer worth living? Even if he's a fraction of the person he once was, he's still alive—and I'm not God.

Fortunately, I don't need to make any life-or-death decisions today. Another type of tube can be snaked through Dad's nose, down into his stomach, allowing him to be rehydrated and nourished while buying time to see if his pneumonia clears and he regains his strength. Unfortunately, the nose tube tends to be unsteady and easy to dislodge, so it works only for a month or so, and only in a hospital setting.

If Dad stabilizes, the J-tube can still be implanted. If he deteriorates, we can remove the nose tube and let him die.

I am my brother's keeper. Everything worth knowing in the teachings of the Torah is embraced in that thought. But no child should have to decide whether to extend a parent's life or end it.

It's not fair. It's not right.

Of course, it happens all the time.

Pop, the Book

September 26, 2005

Dad wakens from a deep sleep and sees me writing beside his bed. His look says, "What's up?"

"I'm writing another book."

Dad's eyes invite me to tell him more.

"Do you know what it's about?" I ask.

"What?"

"You. It's about you. The name of the book is *Life with Pop*."

"No kidding."

He smiles approvingly, then slips back into a world beyond hope or pain.

TERRY SCHIAVO
September 26, 2005

The doctor on duty tries to insert a nose tube and fails. He promises to try again.

I take a break from Dad's bedside and run out to the hot dog truck in the parking lot. Squatting on a low brick wall, I tear into a fat, juicy knockwurst with extra sauerkraut and a squiggle of hot mustard, and chase it down with a fizzy Diet Coke. It shouldn't taste so delicious; Dad hasn't eaten in two days. I pick up my cell and call Donna, Dad's attorney and an expert in elder care.

"I'm totally paralyzed," I confess. "Joel and I can legally refuse Dad the J-tube and let him die. We can also implant it and hope he's glad to be alive. How great would that be? But what if the tube gets implanted and he develops Alzheimer's or has a stroke and turns into a vegetable? What if he says 'enough'—or we say 'enough' for him? Then what?"

"Once the tube is implanted," Donna warns me, "your father may no longer be considered terminal, and a doctor who removes it could be charged with murder. Who's going to take that gamble? Forget promises and handshakes—you need a commitment now, in writing. After the Schiavo case, everyone's scared to death of being sued."

Donna reminds me that just yesterday *The New York*

Times ran a front-page article on doctors who help terminally ill patients end their lives. Only Oregon permits it. "Between us," she says, "a Connecticut doctor would be out of his mind to risk his license or imprisonment. You're a doctor. Would you?"

I toss the last bite of knockwurst in the trash and call the hospital discharge officer. "I want to keep Dad alive," I tell her, "but I can't agree to the J-tube without the right to remove it when death becomes more palatable than life."

The officer offers to research the policies of three nursing homes and get back to me.

"Please, hurry," I plead.

Before I return to Dad, I stop in the ladies' room and scrub the grease from my hands. I've never felt more stuffed or empty. With each passing hour, I'm exquisitely aware that Dad is starving. The doctors can't get the tube down his throat. My unwillingness to approve the more permanent J-tube is depriving him of essential nourishment and medication. I'm sick with anxiety, guilt, and grief. The doctors assure me we still have time, but time is measured in days. Meanwhile, Dad lies there, fading in and out of consciousness, getting weaker, holding on.

Sibling Rivalry
September 27, 2005

How awesome is this responsibility—deciding whether a parent should live or die.

I call Joel with an update on my plans for Dad. "That's crazy," he blurts out, in an uncharacteristic show of anger. "I'm against the J-tube, period. Once it's implanted, I couldn't bring myself to remove it. It would be like murder."

"But if we don't implant one, aren't we killing him?"

"Please, Jan. Let Dad die a natural death. Don't intervene. He's already so sick and frail. Let him go."

"But I had such a sweet visit with him yesterday. He said, 'Aaron and Ali's wedding—wasn't it a wonderful day!' He even asked me if they got their house. Can you imagine?"

"Dad's led a good, full life. It's time."

"What's it to you?" I snap back, overcome with anxiety and doubt. "I take care of him. What does it cost you to let him live a little longer?"

Joel is silent. Then, softly, "I'm not trying to fight with you. We're all worn out—you, me, *and* Dad."

I hang up, burning with anger. Aren't I the one who gets the calls at two in the morning and goes running to the emergency room? Don't I attend to Dad's every need, from pain pills to diapers? I've earned the right to have the final say.

Eventually I simmer down. Anger is so sanctimonious, I remind myself. When we're angry we never think we're wrong—only others can be wrong.

I think about all the patients I've seen over the years who have fought over their elderly parents in the name of love— both the caregivers who felt entitled to make end-of-life decisions, and their siblings, who insisted, "I have a vote; they're my parents, too." How often do these vicious, self-righteous, self-serving arguments rip families apart? It's not a script I want for Joel or me.

As my anger subsides, I feel a creeping sense of shame. Joel loves Dad, too. Who am I to pounce on him for speaking his mind? Am I so sure I know what's right? Neither of us has a stranglehold on truth.

What would Dad want?

"Don't let anything come between you," he would say. "Nothing's that important."

I know that if we let this conflict poison our relationship, we won't be serving Dad. If in our effort to do what's right for him we turn against each other, we will have abandoned him.

I call Joel and apologize. "I'm sorry for what I said. I made it sound as though I'm the better child. I know you love Dad as much as I do, and have his best interest in mind, too."

"We're both trying to do justice to Dad," Joel concedes. "We just can't agree on the form that justice should take."

More Sibling Rivalry

"My eighty-one-year-old mother was just diagnosed with early Alzheimer's," a patient named Kay tells me.

"My sister, Ava, wants Mom to move to Tennessee, close to her, but I think Mom would be happier with her friends in the nursing home near her condo in Hartford. Believe me, it's not Mom Ava's worried about, it's Mom's shrinking assets. The facility she's recommending is dirt cheap."

Kay adjusts the cushions of her chair and moves her capacious Fendi bag off to the side. *"Ava and I have never been that close,"* she admits, *"but these days you could fit the Grand Canyon between us. The other day she said to me, 'I get a vote,' and I said, 'Yes, you do, but I get two votes—one for me and one for Dad. He would want the best for Mom.'"*

"This is a difficult time," I say, empathetically. *"Would it help to know your experience is not so unusual? You'd think that as parents neared the end of their lives their kids would come together, but so often they come to blows, each insisting she alone knows what's best and is acting in the name of love. Siblings who never saw eye to eye when their parents were healthy are bound to lock horns as the anxiety and pressure mount. . . ."*

I ask Kay whether her mother has ever conveyed her wishes or put them in writing.

"She gave us both power of attorney and left it at that," Kay replies. *"But I know she'd live on the street if Ava and I would stop fighting."*

"Would you be willing to meet with your sister and talk through your differences?"

"She's coming to town next week to visit. I could give it a try."

"I recommend you put your own agenda aside and in-

vite her to speak first—it's unlikely she's going to hear your point until she feels you've heard hers. Whatever she says, try to listen with an open heart, and then mirror her, repeating back the essence of her message in your own words, even if you don't agree with her. Watch her face: it sounds obvious, but you'll know you've got it right if she nods her head up and down, as though to say, 'Yes, you've heard me.' Then you can ask her to reverse roles and do the same for you.

"Mirroring is an amazing technique because it allows you both to feel understood and to hear each other's truth and be altered by it. Even if you don't do it exactly right—we're not looking for miracles here—you both may discover that there's more than one version of the truth, and that neither of you is as sick or selfish as the other thinks. You may find out, for instance, that Ava is genuinely crazed about the cost of your mother's care and really does want to see her more. The challenge is to stop defending the rightness of your idea—to get outside your head and open yourself to the possibility that your sister's position may be reasonable, too. If the two of you do this, you're more likely to come up with a solution that works for both of you.

"Here's another thought. Siblings often think they're fighting about something that's happening today—should we put Mom in this facility or that, should we approve this medical procedure or that—but what they're really doing is restaging unresolved childhood battles, and tearing at old wounds. You may need to go back in time in order to go forward and resolve the current conflict."

"Our differences have deep roots. Where would we begin?"

"You can ask Ava, 'I'm wondering if I did something over the years that poisoned the space between us and makes it hard for us to agree on Mom's care today.' If she's a conflict avoider, she may deny there's a problem. You could press her by saying, 'If we don't air our grievances, they'll always sit between us. I'm asking you to be honest with me. Please tell me if something is bothering you.' Then be prepared to listen. Don't be surprised if old resentments, long suppressed, erupt to the surface: 'Mom always treated your kids better than mine.' 'You were always her favorite.' 'Why were you given the beach house?' 'You always needed to be in control.' 'You were always too busy, too selfish, to help out—why should you get a vote now?'"

"The conflict sometimes gets played out between siblings when it's really between parent and child. A daughter who shut her mother out of her life, for example, may, in the end, insist on keeping her mother alive at any cost—one last chance to say, 'I really do love you.' A son, denied the parental attention he craved as a child, may register his bitterness by voting 'Do Not Resuscitate.' Siblings can claw at each other without having a clue what they're fighting about. Is that what's going on with you and Ava?"

"There's a lot of baggage between us. A lot of garbage. Ava has always had an easier time with Mom. And I got along better with Dad. I'm sure she has feelings about that. I know I do. There's also a big discrepancy in

our finances—I'm much more comfortable than she is. If I were honest, though, I'd have to admit I feel as threatened by Mom's expenses as Ava does."

"Sometimes family secrets make it impossible to resolve conflicts. It may be helpful to unlock them and deal with them directly."

"Actually, I know something Ava doesn't know I know. Last year I secretly went through Mom's old checkbooks and found out she gave Ava $10,000 a year for at least four years. I was shocked. Hurt. So maybe I'm irked that Ava won't cough up the dough for Mom."

"Would it help to confess your secret?"

"I don't know. I'm embarrassed because I had no right to rifle through Mom's personal records. But the secret weighs on me and probably affects me more than I realize."

"It's hard enough making end-of-life decisions by yourself, never mind making them with your siblings. So be prepared. This is a time of high emotion. There are so many feelings to confront, so many to deny. So many words not said. Too many words, the wrong words, that could be spoken with a venomous tongue. And so much personal meaning assigned to each other's positions. But if you try to hear each other out and address the unacknowledged subtext of your fight, you may satisfy your mother's wish to see her children at peace with each other before she dies."

Kay leaves, and I think of my own strained relationship with my brother. When did I become such an expert in sibling conflicts?

DNR
September 27, 2005

"Do you want us to write 'DNR'—Do Not Resuscitate—on your father's chart?" the nurse asks me.

"Yes." I could be signing up for HBO.

I'm in a bookstore later in the day, flipping through magazines, when I come across an article on why we should discard DNR—not the principle that preserves the parent's right to refuse care, but the loaded language that implies neglect and abandonment and turns the child into an executioner. The author, Marianne Dekker Mattera, proposes instead the acronym AND—Allow Natural Death.

I agree.

DNR says, "Do not bring back." AND says, "Let nature take its course." DNR says, "Do not save or rescue—leave the wounded on the battlefield and the stroke victim lying in the street." AND says, "Let life have its way."

Mattera has nothing but contempt for the doctors who fought to save her mother from a massive cerebral hemorrhage. The assumption that we must always intervene, and defy death, robbed Mattera and her mother of a peaceful good-bye.

HUMAN ERRORS
September 27–28, 2005

Without a nose tube, Dad will die. He can't last on an IV drip alone. As he dozes, a new ENT doctor whisks into the room, effortlessly glides a tube up Dad's nose, examines him, and slips it out.

"Wait!" I yowl.

"No problem to reinsert it," he assures me. And he strolls out of the room.

I can't believe what I've seen. The cocky bastard. I understand that specialists work in teams, covering for each other, but is it too much to ask him to read his patient's chart? I want to get even. I want him to suffer and starve, like Dad.

Later, the doctor calls to tell me he tried again and failed. "Your father became agitated and wouldn't take the tube," he says. "I'll be back tomorrow."

I hang up, furious at this arrogant bungler for refusing to apologize and making Dad the problem. You don't need a medical degree to know Dad is not going to accept a tube awake and without sedation.

Another day passes. Dad, still without a nose tube, is moved into the next room. An oxygen line dangles from his lap.

"What's this?" I ask the nurse.

"Oh," she says contritely, quickly reattaching it to an outlet. "That's my fault. I didn't hook it up. I'm so sorry."

"Your honesty is refreshing," I say, and mean it. In this world of starched white coats, it's reassuring when someone has the humility and confidence to admit their mistakes. Screwups are a way of life in hospitals—they're easier to forgive when the staff doesn't try to blame the patient.

UNSPOKEN WORDS
September 28, 2005

The doctor calls again. "I asked your father if he wants a nose tube," he reports, "and he said no. It's all in his chart."

I try to imagine their conversation. Dad may have said no to the tube—who would want one?—but did he realize he was saying no to life? No one—not the doctors, not the social workers, not the loving son, not even I, the seasoned psychologist and primary caregiver—has had the courage or decency to tell Dad he can't swallow food or his own secretions, and without some sort of feeding tube, he won't survive.

It's time to talk to Dad about his options. Ask his opinion. Find out whether he wants us to stop treating him or fight to prolong his life. Help him, should he want to live, to imagine what lies ahead.

How can a parent be expected to convey his dying wishes if he doesn't know how close he is to death?

It's time for a heart-to-heart.

THE *D* WORD
September 29, 2005

I'm at the hospital by nine. My heart is pounding—and breaking.

Dad lies stiffly in bed, unable to lift his head, so I draw my face up close to his and take his hand. We spend a few minutes chitchatting, warming up. *He may not be alert for long, so you'd better get into it now.*

"Dad," I say gingerly, "we need to have a serious talk about what's happening to you."

He seems to be listening with every nerve in his body. I speak as slowly and gently as I know how, for his sake, and mine. "The reason you got pneumonia is because when you swallow, the food drips into your lungs."

I look into his eyes to see if he's registering what I'm saying. He's with me every step of the way.

"You can't eat anymore or you'll get sick. You need a feeding tube. Do you understand?"

Dad licks his parched lips, fumbling for the right words, then responds with perfect clarity, "Yes, I do."

"Repeat back to me what I'm telling you so I know you understand."

"I can't eat by my mouth. I need a feeding tube."

"That's right."

I'm amazed and relieved at his level of functioning. Then he asks, "For how long?"

Oh my. This poor man. He really doesn't understand how sick he is. How could he? He's been in and out of hospitals his whole life. Why should he assume this round is any different? How would he know his illness is incurable?

I turn back and look him straight in the face. "Forever, Dad. You'll need a feeding tube forever. You'll never eat food again. Maybe a few bites of applesauce or soup, but mostly you'll eat from a feeding tube."

I move away from the bed, wiping my eyes, trying to hide the evidence of my aching sadness. *This is his decision, Jan. Don't confuse him with your emotions.*

"Does Joel know?" Dad asks.

"Yes."

"What does he say?"

What do I tell him? That Joel said no to any intervention? Is that fair to Joel? Would Dad understand? Would he want to know?

"Joel has mixed feelings about it," I say, sidestepping the truth.

"Can I think about it for a day?" Dad asks. The innocence of his request chokes me. This is a man who never asks for anything. It is his life we are talking about.

"Of course you can." I cradle his hand. "It's a very big decision."

I have yet to mention the *D* word. It's time. I bring it up obliquely. "Do you ever think about dying?"

"All the time."

I'm shocked. Dad has never discussed death with me before. I reach for words and come up empty-handed. Dad closes his eyes and slips away.

When I return in the afternoon, Dad is no longer capable of a sustained conversation, much less a talk about life and death. The day passes. As he shifts in and out of consciousness, I climb into bed with him. He lies on his back, covered with thin blankets, his head propped up on pillows. An oxygen tube hangs from a nostril. The other remains free to receive sustenance, or not. I snuggle up to this sweet teddy bear of a man and caress his bruised, lumpy arms, swollen from innumerable blood tests and IV fluid.

"Pop," I whisper, kissing his rough, stubbled cheek, "you've always been a man who cries easily, with no shame. I can't understand why you don't cry now. Are you at peace with where you are, or lost in a morphine high? It would be so much easier if you would tell me what to do. Please, tell me what you want me to do."

INDECISION

September 30, 2005

Can we legally remove a J-tube? No word yet. In the meantime, the doctors sedate Dad and manage to snake a temporary tube down his nose. It's held in place by a thick strip of masking tape drawn horizontally across his face. Dad doesn't complain. He doesn't even seem to know it's there.

The tube gives me—us—a brief reprieve, but I'm left with the unbearable task of deciding Dad's fate. Turning to Jewish law for direction, I learn that human life is sacred and must be preserved. Once a stomach tube is implanted, it cannot be removed to expedite death. On the other hand, if a patient cannot be cured, extraordinary intervention (for example, an antibiotic for recurrent infection) is not required. Food and water, though, are not considered extraordinary, and therefore must be provided.

So what would Dad say? He's not particularly religious, although he loves a good matzo ball soup. He *is* eminently practical. He cherishes life but not more than he hates sickness and suffering.

Pleasure. Pain. How do you weigh them against each other? How much pleasure does it take to want to live? How much suffering to want to die?

Choose life for Dad? Of course. Some people are born

buoyant, generally content with whatever life sends their way. Dad is one of them. He doesn't need wild adventures to make a day worth living. When the pain is manageable, being alive is enough. And life, even with a J-tube, would afford some simple pleasures. Summerwood wouldn't let him back, so he would have to live out his days in a nursing home, away from his buddies, but Joel and I would visit him, and so would his grandchildren from time to time. He couldn't eat, but he would get nourishment through the tube and wouldn't starve. He could still watch Tiger hit an eagle at Augusta, and cheer the Huskies on. He could still hear blue eyes crooning, and the best of Lady Day. So many special moments to live for, so many ordinary, everyday moments to live for.

Choose death for Dad? Let him go? It seems the merciful thing to do. Sores—compression wounds—have begun to form on his lower back and shoulder from pressing against his wheelchair and bed, where he's doomed to spend most of his day. Increasingly, even sitting or lying down is uncomfortable. He can hardly swallow. More and more often he awakens in the middle of the night, gagging on his secretions. It's just a matter of time before he gets pneumonia again. Meanwhile, his cancer continues to metastasize to his bones, and arthritis has moved into his right hip joint, held together by a pin. This can't be fun.

For Dad, being alive and living aren't the same. Quality of life matters to him. And Dad's sources of pleasure are drying up: no more food, that primal pleasure. No more trips to Elizabeth Park—hoisting him in and out of a wheelchair has become a nightmare for everyone. Will he make new friends? I imagine him sitting in his wheelchair, strapped in like his old friend Arthur, curled forward in front of a TV he can't see or control, peeing into a diaper. *How much can a person's life shrink and still retain its shape and meaning?*

As I peer into Dad's future, trying to weigh the good times against the bad, I wonder: how many moments of pleasure in a day of sleep or suffering make life worth living? If a person dozes seventy-five percent of the time, is delusional ten percent of the time, cogent but miserable ten percent of the time, happy, truly consciously happy five percent of the time, who is to say his life is not good, and worth living?

Back and forth I go—life, death, life, death—like a metronome. I don't know what's right for Dad. I don't know whether letting him live is prolonging his life or prolonging his dying. What I do know is that there's no perfect solution, and that unless I can accept something less absolute and certain I'll never resolve my ambivalence, and never be able to act on his behalf.

Joan

At eighty-seven, Joan, a former high school English teacher, qualifies as my oldest patient. Her Jamaican aide, LaShelle, drives her to her appointment every six weeks or so. I watch her help Joan out of the car and support her as she trudges up the steps. Since her stroke, Joan moves tentatively, using a cane. Once inside my office, she extricates herself from her coat, takes a seat, and waves good-bye to LaShelle.

"*Come back at ten, okay?*" *I tell her. LaShelle smiles and nods. She knows the routine.*

I turn to Joan. "*So how are you?*"

"*I'm doing well, actually,*" *she says proudly, pulling herself up a few inches in her chair.* "*On most days, I still have my mind. I can still put together a sentence and not embarrass myself. I'm not in pain most of the time. I consider myself lucky.*"

"*That's all good to hear.*"

"*The hardest thing is that I can no longer read. The stroke did something to my eyesight. I used to love to read. Books have always been a wonderful source of comfort and stimulation. But I'm trying to make the best of it. I 'prepare a face to meet the faces that you meet,'*" *she recites, smiling, looking pleased.*

"*You're amazing,*" *I say, sincerely.* "*Your mind is strong, and you look pretty good, too.*"

"*LaShelle dresses me. You know, I'm required to have twenty-four-hour care now. I don't think I need it, but they tell me I can't stay at Maplewood without it. It's a terrible invasion of privacy, even though LaShelle is very pleasant. I hate having someone hover over me, listening to every conversation. I hate feeling pressured to be upbeat or friendly when all I want is to be left alone.*"

"*Does she have to be in the room with you every minute? Would you like me to talk to her?*"

"*If you could do it without insulting her, that would be great,*" *Joan replies.* "*And the whole thing is costing a fortune. Thousands of dollars. For what? I feel bad, eat-*

ing up my children's inheritance. Sometimes I think I'm worth more to them dead than alive."

"*Joan, your kids are making their own way in the world. I'm sure they're happy you're safe and comfortable. And if they're not? The money is yours. You and your husband worked hard for it. Besides, you supported them their whole lives and just gave them your Cape house. If you don't leave them another penny, you've given them plenty."*

Joan gets solemn. "Right now, you know, I live in a condo in a continuing-care facility. There's an Alzheimer's unit and a nursing home a few buildings away. Yesterday, I asked LaShelle to take me to see it. The place is clean, although you can't help smelling something sour in the air. The staff tries, and is friendly. But the people—God help me—stare out vacantly into space, with tubes coming in and out of every orifice of their bodies. It's not living. Not for me. I pray every night that God will be merciful and take me before I get there. I pray, 'Please take me in the night when I'm asleep.' And I don't even believe in God."

"*It sounds as though your biggest fear isn't dying."*

"*That's right. For me, when you're dead, you're dead. I don't believe in an afterlife. This is it. But I'm terrified of sickness and pain. Most of all, I'm terrified of being trapped in my body with no ability to pull the plug."*

"*Do your kids know your wishes?"*

"*I've been very clear, but they don't like me to talk about it." She wets her lips. "May I have a glass of water?"*

"*Sure." I go into the kitchen and come back with a*

quarter of a cup. Joan takes a sip, her hand jerking, then goes on. "A friend of mine is in the nursing home. She stopped eating, but they gave her intravenous. I think she wants to die, but they jump-started her again. What's the point?"

"If you'd like, I can check with your kids and Maplewood, and make sure they know your wishes, and that all the paperwork is in order."

"Yes, that's good. When I leave here, I don't remember half of what we talked about. It's nice having an advocate who listens to me and takes me seriously."

I've taken notes throughout our session, and shortly before it ends, I call LaShelle into my office and go over a list of to-dos.

- *Lashelle will go to the library at Maplewood and see if they have Books on Tape.*
- *I'll call Joan's children and Maplewood, and make sure they know her end-of-life instructions, and have written and signed documents on hand.*
- *There's a new "mindful meditation" group at Maplewood that teaches residents to relax their muscles, clear their minds, breathe. LaShelle will sign Joan up.*
- *Joan would like some privacy, some time alone. When she's on the living room phone, LaShelle will sit in the hallway with the door slightly ajar, or in the bedroom, checking on Joan periodically.*

- *LaShelle will take Joan to the clinic to see about the sore on her wrist that's not healing.*
- *Joan wants to put together a family scrapbook. LaShelle will help her.*

That's it for today. LaShelle and I help Joan into her coat and return her safely to her car. I give her a hug. "It's good to see you," I say. "Be well."

"It's good to see you, too," she answers. "I hope to be back in a month."

I watch the car disappear down the driveway and head back into my office. I need to prepare for the next patient, but Joan lingers in my mind. As a psychologist and daughter of an aging parent, I want to help her. But how can I? What words of wisdom do I have to offer? Sometimes a patient has negative thoughts that are distorted or exaggerated. I can help them see things more accurately. But Joan's fears are real and justified. What comfort can I provide? I don't have answers, but I can listen patiently, respectfully, and make sure her wishes are followed. I can coordinate her care. I can make sure her voice is heard. I can lighten her burden, reduce her anxiety, and help her leave this world with dignity and style.

The Shame of Money
October 1, 2005

Profiting from a parent's death—how low can a child go?
Yet who doesn't dream of inheriting a pile of money? Who
doesn't wonder, "How much?"

I never expected a cent from my parents. Dad would die
first, and Mom, I was sure, would outlive their savings. But
now a small inheritance is imaginable. I sit at the kitchen
table, flipping through my little green accounting book, com-
puting my windfall, and dreaming of ways of spending it.

The pool Michael and I just built—Dad's remaining assets would pay for it, as well as a new septic system and
driveway. A bathroom in the basement office? Done. And
those fabulous earrings I admired at Bergdorf's? No problem. I'm giddy as I wander the aisles of Saks and Barneys on
an imaginary shopping spree.

Wouldn't it be great, also, to pass on some of this wealth
to my children and my grandchildren? To invest a share in
my retirement so I could afford caregivers of my own someday, and not burden my kids? The possibilities make my
head spin. Except I'd have to deal with the ghoulish reality
that my inheritance was contingent on Dad's death.

The phone rings. It's Dad's gerontologist, Mary King,
calling to check how he's doing. The director of geriatric

services at Hartford Hospital, she's everything a doctor should be: compassionate, attentive, influential, and wise.

"May I tell you what I'm struggling with?" I ask, grateful for a chance to confess the dark truth. "I think that since I'll profit financially when Dad dies, I can't allow myself to let him go. I'd be trading him in to line my own pockets, and that's just too sick, too evil to contemplate. So I'm doing everything possible to keep him alive, even if that means denying him a humane exit. It's perverse, the money thing. It's warping my capacity to think clearly about what's best for Dad."

Poor Dr. King: she's getting an earful—more than she bargained for. She never signed on as my psychologist.

"These decisions are always hard," she reassures me, without a hint of condescension.

"I can't trust my own motivations," I go on. "I don't know whether letting Dad die is merciful or reprehensible. Loving or greedy. Pulling the plug feels like murder, with a cash prize."

THE CONSULTATION
October 3, 2005

As Michael and I turn into the temple parking lot for Rosh Hashanah services, my cell phone rings. It's Dr. King. "There's going to be a meeting about your dad today at one-thirty," she announces. "I'll be there, along with a few others involved in his care. We'd like to talk through our findings and recommendations. Can you make it?"

"Of course."

I call Michael's sister and tell her we're coming to Hartford. We'll swing by after the meeting.

"They're going to recommend hospice," she alerts me.

Hospice? It never occurred to me. Hospice is the last stop before the grave, the place you go to die.

In the sanctuary, Rabbi Stein tells the story of a young architect who has plans for a state-of-the-art synagogue. He boasts to his mother about how many seats it will hold, how many books the library will shelve, how well-equipped the classrooms will be. "I'm proud of you," his mother says. "But is it a place where you can go to cry?"

So many of us are in temple today, the start of the Jewish New Year, to cry. I cry for Dad, such a good man, and for his life, hanging by a thread. I cry for myself when I think of living in a world without him. I cry because I cry so easily. It feels good, a good cry.

Jewish tradition teaches that between now and Yom Kippur—the Days of Awe—God will decide who is inscribed in the Book of Life for the coming year. The timing is eerie. "Please, God," I pray, "if you give Dad life, give him the health to enjoy it. Let him laugh again. If you strike his name, take him swiftly, painlessly in the night. And help me do what's best for him."

Mourners rise to recite Kaddish, the prayer for the dead. Next week, next year, I'll be standing with them, my tears on display, honoring Dad.

Michael and I leave early for the hospital. Dr. King greets us with the news: none of the rehab facilities—not even the one she directs—will agree in writing to let us remove the J-tube, should we choose to implant it. "We're operating in a climate of fear," she explains. "I'm sorry."

I'm surprised, but not greatly. We were told to expect this. Before I can process the implications, we're ushered into a dark, wood-paneled boardroom. A pride of doctors and aides is assembled around a large oval table, waiting for us. I feel outnumbered. One by one, they introduce themselves and state their relationship to Dad. The mood is somber, formal, surreal. Dad, I learn, has developed pulmonary edema. His hands, scrotum, and feet have ballooned with liquid.

A new doctor has taken over Dad's case. He looks too young to be in charge of an eighty-five-year-old man, too inexperienced to be making end-of-life decisions. He speaks deliberately, with an air of authority, as though to compensate for his tender years: "I question where we're going with your father," he says. "We can probably clear up the pneumonia and the edema. If your father gets stronger, we may be able to insert a permanent feeding tube. But in the end, his basic condition remains. Your father cannot swallow, and the likelihood of his developing pneumonia again and returning to the hospital is high."

His eyes bore into mine. His exact words escape me, but their message is clear—"Why extend Dad's life? Anyone with a sense of compassion would let him go."

The others nod in agreement, or stare away. Dad has now been on IV for ten days. He sleeps most of the time, eyes closed. His heart pumps irregularly. Thanks to morphine, he doesn't appear to be in pain, but his breathing is heavy. He eats through his nose and drinks through his veins. I haven't seen the nurse suck up the fluids trapped in his throat, but I can imagine the horror. What exactly is the point of rescuing him?

Michael slowly reviews our options with the medical staff. He's buying me time to take it all in.

I ask the doctor, "If we disconnect the nose tube and put Dad in hospice, where would he go?"

"We have hospice here in the hospital, but frankly your father is too sick to be moved. He could stay right on this floor."

Too sick to be moved to hospice? This really defines the moment.

My brain scrambles to make a final decision. Why equivocate any longer? There's nothing more to know. I feel pressured, though, and suspicious. Why should I listen to these experts? What do they care about Dad? Maybe the discharge officer is lazy and wants to avoid the hassle of finding Dad a home. And the social worker? Would her world be rocked if Dad were kicked off the planet? This young, new doctor, what does he know about Dad and all he has endured—how treasured he is, the formidable space his absence will create in my life? Am I going to let him intimidate me? He sees a sick old man. Maybe he believes Dad's hospital bed could be better used by someone younger and healthier, a more valuable, productive member of society, with many more years of life ahead of him. Isn't this the prevailing argument for rationing health care today—that too much money is being spent on the old and irremediably sick—money down the drain?

I look around the room. These people have already met and made up their minds. There are no surprises for them, no answers they haven't heard before.

I turn to Michael. "What do you think?"

"I'd let him go."

I look beseechingly at Dr. King. "The choice is yours," she says sympathetically.

I sit like a stump, ready to be told what to do, ready to put the decision into someone else's scrubbed hands.

I feel scared, unsure. Tired. Relieved. Decades of collective wisdom are gathered at this table. These responsible, decent, well-intentioned people have all voted to end Dad's life. Aren't they trying to help me do what's right for him? They may even care about me, the devoted, depleted daughter.

Or they may not care about me, or Dad, at all. The doctors may simply be telling it as it is: your father is sick. He will only get sicker. There is no cure. He's resting peacefully. Why put him through more?

"I'm pretty sure we're going to let Dad die," I hear myself say, "but I'd like to speak to my brother first."

"That's fine," Dr. King says slowly, setting the pace. I look into her warm eyes and blink back an ocean of tears.

Alone in the hallway, I call Joel. "I'm here with the hospital staff," I tell him. "They're recommending we let Dad go."

I find myself repeating the words he spoke to me just last week: Dad has had a good life and is never going to get better, only worse. All that lies ahead for him in this world is pain, and more pain.

The words feel right, right enough.

"Okay."

I hold the phone in silence, just to be sure, just in case there's something more to say, and then press "end."

Nothing can soften the moment.

HOSPICE
October 5, 2005

Dad's trip to hospice takes him two doors down the hallway to a spacious, private room. With its pastel walls, drained of color, and matching floral chairs, we could be in a Holiday Inn. Near Dad's bed sits a vase of creamy spider mums, a gift from the guys at Summerwood. On a table, a hospital still life: a box of Kleenex, a pitcher of water, a stack of paper cups.

Through the large picture window the sun is making its daily rounds. Dad, oblivious, lies on his back, eyes shut, tucked in between layers of soft cotton blankets. The nose tube is gone. Morphine drips into his veins, numbing his senses.

I pass time canceling medical appointments Dad no longer needs: surgery to remove the tumor on his ear, a biannual checkup at the VA, an injection to contain his prostate cancer, a trip to the dentist to fix a broken tooth. I call the director of Summerwood and arrange to vacate his apartment. I don't know what to do with myself. I don't know what to do first.

A young woman, too young to be here, walks in and introduces herself as a palliative-care doctor. Her job is not to make Dad better but to make him more comfortable as he gets worse. She checks his vital signs as tenderly as a mother.

She is attuned to me, as well, and senses my anxiety. "Your father has declined rapidly since we stopped his life support," she observes. "That shows he was ready to die and wouldn't have lasted long, whatever we did. You made the right decision to let him go."

Kind words. They may be what palliative-care doctors are trained to say, but they're what I need to hear.

"Do you want your father to continue to receive his daily medication?" she asks. Dad still takes pills to control his cholesterol, his blood pressure, his Parkinson's.

I shake my head no.

"Then he'll just receive the morphine."

The doctor makes a note on her chart, asks if I need anything, and leaves.

I'm alone with Dad again. He gurgles and pulls heavily at the air; otherwise, the room is stone silent. No one comes in. No one tells me what to do. I walk around the bed, from side to side, shrinking back from him, this pale, pasty stranger, as though death were contagious. He looks gaunt, maybe twenty pounds lighter than when he bit into his last tuna fish sandwich a week or two ago. His flesh collects in bags under his eyes. *Go ahead,* I coach myself. *He's your father.* I pull a chair up to the mattress, as close to him as I can get, and nestle his hand in mine. His warmth flows through me. I hold on.

So is this it? Is this all there is? I never imagined the end could be so effortless, so civilized, so matter-of-fact.

Hospice, I realize, is as much for the caregiver as it is for the dying.

A Visit from Sister Sue
October 6, 2005

Sister Sue joins me at Dad's bedside, as she promised.

"Hi, honey," she says, wrapping her arms around me. "How are you holding up?"

"Okay."

I'm not okay. I've never felt more alone, or scattered. But it's comforting to see her caring face.

She pulls up a chair beside me, close to Dad. He doesn't stir.

"It's a special friend who comes to hospice to hang out with you and your dying father," I whisper.

"What's family for?"

Aides come and go, pouring tea, massaging Dad's limbs. I'm touched by their beneficence. Do I have them to thank, or death?

"How about some music?" an aide asks. "They say a person's hearing is the last sense to go."

"Dad loves Frank Sinatra."

"Sinatra it is," she says, closing the door softly behind her.

I try to imagine listening to *A Swingin' Affair!* while Dad lies on his deathbed. It seems disrespectful, sacrilegious even, but how could it be if it lightens his journey and distracts us from our grief?

"I'm going for lunch," Sue announces. "What can I get you?"

I protest, she insists, and before long she's back from the cafeteria with a plastic container of tuna fish salad and a pecan brownie. From such unremembered gifts are lifelong friendships made.

Sue stays a couple of hours, reminiscing about the time she accompanied her mother and father down this same weary path. She loved and lost her parents, too, and life went on.

"You'll get through this," she says, hugging me good-bye. "We all do."

I'm glad to be alone again with Dad. I need some quiet time to gather my thoughts and feelings and find my bearings. He lies on his back, eyes sealed. His heavy, raspy breathing fills the room.

Taking a cue from the aides, I gently knead Dad's hands and feet. Then I climb into his bed, drape my arm across his wasted belly, and press my wet face against his pale cheek. It's dry, remarkably dry.

"Hi there, Pop," I whisper in his ear. "It's Janis Sheri."

Dad raises his eyebrows, not enough to open his eyes, but high. I'm shocked. I cup his bloated fingers in my hands and gently squeeze them. He squeezes back and holds on—tightly.

"I hear you, Pop," I reassure him. "I hear you. What's to say? What haven't we said that needs to be said now? You were a great husband to Mom and a great dad to me and Joel. You'll be in my heart forever. I love you."

I look at the clock. Two-thirty. I have a patient at five. If I leave now, I can make it home in time. I'll come back tonight and camp out with Dad for the next few days.

On the road, I occupy myself with details—canceling Dad's phone and newspaper subscription, calling family and friends. When I open the front door, the phone is ringing.

It's the nurse.

Dad is dead.

What? What was I thinking? For five years, I watched over him, every step of the way—how could I have abandoned him at the final hour? I knew he was dying, but somehow I didn't get it. I thought we had more time.

I sit in my office, staring out the window at the darkening sky. The doorbell rings. I let my patient in. I'll deal with myself later. I have nothing now but time.

Regret

Four years have passed since I last saw Felicia, a single, middle-aged woman with a big heart. She sits in my office, telling me her sad story.

"When my father died—that's where we left off—I moved back home to live with Mom. At first she tried not to lean on me, but last year she was diagnosed with breast cancer and had to undergo a radical, bilateral mastectomy and four months of chemotherapy. She was so weak and nauseous, she didn't have the strength to lift herself out of bed. Last week she died."

Felicia recounts the complicated medical procedures

she took her mother through, the costs she underwrote to cure her, her decision to move her mother into hospice when all else failed.

"The last day, I rubbed Mom's hands and feet with her favorite moisturizing cream and sang an Irish lullaby she used to sing to me as a child. She seemed pretty comfortable. She would doze off, then wake up and see me by her side, and smile. We had a great day together. Then I ran home to feed Juniper, my cat, and before I could open the can the doctor called to tell me Mom had had a stroke and died. My God, how could I have left her, even for a second?"

"Felicia," I begin tentatively, "what did you do that was so awful—run off to feed your cat? Wasn't this just one more act of caregiving? You were probably so frazzled, so overcome with grief, you thought death would wait for you."

"Do you think Mom gave up because *I left?"*

"So many people die when caregivers step away— eighty-five percent, a hospice worker told me—it could be your mother wanted to die alone, the way some people want to sleep alone. Maybe she was afraid of spoiling your last memory of her, and wanted to spare you more pain. Or maybe it was just her time. We'll never know. If we could bring her back into this room right now, what do you think she'd say to you?"

"She'd probably say, 'You've been a wonderful daughter. You're always so hard on yourself and never feel you do enough for people. Go take care of yourself. I'm fine.'"

"Felicia, that compassionate voice—call it your

mother's or your own—is asking you, 'Why focus on the one moment you weren't there for her and ignore the count-less hours you spent taking her for treatments, feeding her, coddling her when she was sick?' You gave her so much love, so much of your best self—you would never con-demn a friend as heartlessly as you condemn yourself."

I stumble on. "It's not easy taking care of an aging parent. There's always so much more that can be done. There are always regrets."

My eyes cloud over. My patient is touched by my tears. What she doesn't know, what I don't tell her, is that I'm crying for both of us.

A GOOD MAN DIES
October 7, 2005

I know the routine. Contact the Abraham Greene Mortuary and Rabbi Stein, order another plain pine casket, and swing by the cemetery to check out the plot. The same damn garbage can sits a yard from the gravesite, overflowing with trash. I drag it down the broken concrete walk, cursing, re-minding myself that there's no point getting all worked up, some things never change.

Tomorrow, Dad will be buried next to Mom. They'll be a couple again. Rabbi Stein will pin a black ribbon to my chest, rip it, and say, "With great love there is great loss."

The service will be small—almost none of Dad's friends are alive or well enough to attend. But our family will be there, the next in line, and those who follow; and after the coffin is lowered into the ground and splattered with dirt, we'll return home to sit shiva. Honoring Jewish tradition, we'll wash the spirits of the dead from our hands before entering the house, and then bite into hard-boiled eggs, a symbol of our willingness to take up life again.

Dad is gone, but I can honor his memory by emulating the qualities I love most in him—his ability to find humor in everyday life, his delight in nature, his talent for bringing out the best in people, his refusal to get ruffled by nonsense. And his love of a good sandwich. I owe him that, while I still have the stomach and teeth to chow it down.

Dear Pop. There's no great accomplishment here, no extraordinary legacy. What you said about Mom when she died is exactly what I'd like to say about you: I want the world to know, a good man died. A good man.

On Growing Old
October 16, 2005

We grow up when we lose our parents. In facing their mortality, we face our own. Suddenly, we're orphans with no one to shield us from the finiteness of our lives. There's no hiding from it—our turn is next.

When I think of my inexorable decline, first losing a life partner, then losing life itself, I cringe. Fortunately, having cared for Dad, I feel more prepared for what lies ahead, as though I've taken a course in being a good Old Person. Thanks to him, I have a better sense of what it takes to morph gracefully into elderdom.

What exactly have I learned? Here's a list of reminders that may help me survive old age and be the kind of model octogenarian my friends and family will want to have around. I plan to file it away in a drawer. If I'm lucky, I'll live long enough to need it, and remember where it is.

- Be sure to show appreciation when your kids extend themselves to you. They have so much competing for their time. Don't take those Eskimo Pies in the freezer for granted; they didn't just magically appear.
- Make your health-care wishes known to your kids with the utmost specificity. Don't saddle them with this responsibility, or you may find yourself dining on kosher fluid piped into your belly, against your will. Your input will free them from having to make these onerous and morbid decisions on their own.
- Don't be ashamed to use a cane or walker. It's dumb to let vanity trip you up. It's selfish, too, because your children will need to manage your recovery.
- Don't criticize yourself for wanting to steal bananas from the dining room, or for worrying about the cost of fruit salad. It's an age-appropriate preoccupation.
- Assign power of attorney to those you trust, and let them know how you'd like your money invested and

your assets distributed. It's sticky business when these decisions are in their hands without directives from you.

- Don't be too proud to pee in a diaper. It beats sitting in soggy pants and allows you to travel in wider circles.
- Tell your friends and family how much you love them, and how proud you are of them. You may not be able to find the words tomorrow.
- Redress old injuries. Invite your kids and close friends to air their grievances and tell you how you've hurt them over the years. Listen with an open heart. If you've wronged them, have the courage to apologize. Then, work to forgive yourself.
- Inhale the moment, often, every day. Don't wait until your eyesight or hearing is compromised to realize your blessings. Use your senses to imbibe the wonder of the world.
- Don't let others make you feel you're more trouble than you're worth. Your life is precious, no matter how impaired, if it's precious to you.
- Don't be cranky and demanding. You'll lose your audience.
- Remember your kids' birthdays. Write them in your calendar or ask your aide to remind you. You're not the only one who likes to be celebrated.
- Sign up for activities. Try new ones. They will make your life more interesting and make *you* more interesting.
- Call friends. No one wants to be your social director, always reaching out to you.

- If your partner predeceases you, you might try dating. Dying of loneliness won't bring that person back. Forming new attachments won't diminish your love for him, or her.
- Eat tuna fish sandwiches in a garden. Watch the bees. Smell the roses. Find pleasure in the small stuff.
- Don't be angry at your kids for putting you in a home. They may feel closer to you if they have their own space. Conversely, don't rush to accept an invitation to live with them; they may be extending themselves for the wrong reasons.
- Your mind will play tricks on you. Be prepared. If you think your caregivers are treating you poorly and ripping you off, don't be afraid to speak up to someone who can look into the matter and protect you. But be careful not to bite the hand that feeds you. If you don't have facts, report your fears without harsh accusations.
- Be prepared to resent the invasion of privacy, the infantilization, that comes with having an aide. Try to negotiate some boundaries (or ask your kids to intervene) to balance your need for safety and assistance against your need for an autonomous life.
- Don't be bashful about wearing a hearing aid. It beats sitting in silence—unless it doesn't.
- Don't let your bones calcify in bed or in a chair. Walk the hallways or the pool, move your legs, flap your arms. Use your lungs. Get outdoors even for a few minutes every day.

- Take care of your appearance. Don't let yourself smell or rot. Ask people you trust to tell you what needs attending to.
- Don't abuse drugs to control your pain, help you sleep, or medicate your depression. They'll only make you more miserable and unstable.
- Be patient with your caregivers. It's a hellish job.
- Try to accept your decline with humor. At ninety-two, Robert Maxwell mused, "As I look over my life, I have many regrets. Fortunately, I don't remember what they are."
- Stay sharp: read the paper, do puzzles, play bridge.
- There will come a time when you'll need to give up your driver's license and car. Better to do this too soon than too late.
- Your memory and strength will fade. Don't let that happen to your enthusiasm for life. Find something amazing about each day.
- When bad things happen and there's nothing you can do to change them, try to adopt an attitude of acceptance. *Rome, shmome.*
- Be careful not to pit one child against another. Let them know that you never want them to fight over you, that nothing matters more than for them to remain a supportive and loving presence in each other's lives.
- Ask your kids to tell you the truth about your health. You may want to opt for comfort and maintenance, not cure.

- Be diligent about taking your medications. Don't skip doses or make changes without consulting your caregiver.
- Convey your wishes regarding your funeral arrangements. Do you want to die in a hospital or at home? What clothes do you want to be buried in? What do you want your obituary to say? Where do you want charitable contributions sent? It's your last party. The more information you convey, the more likely it will go your way.
- Ask your family to level with you when you're dying. If possible, tell them when you're ready to go.

Days of Awe
October 3, 2005

Sunset, erev Rosh Hashanah. The start of the Jewish New Year, a time of repentance and renewal. As Rabbi Stein extols the virtues of caregivers, I recall a passage from the *mahzor*, the Jewish prayer book: "Days are like scrolls. Write thereon only what you want to have remembered about you."